George III

THE BRITISH LIBRARY
HISTORIC LIVES

George III

Christopher Wright

The British Library

Acknowledgements

'Now, what I want is, Facts ... Facts alone are wanted in life.' So declares Mr Gradgrind in Charles Dickens's novel *Hard Times*. If only it were that simple. Alas, interpretation is of equal importance. It can turn facts on their head and transform them into quite other facts. However, in so far as it is possible to speak of facts in history, I have relied in this account on both contemporary records and the work of many subsequent historians. Sadly, it has only been possible to refer to a few of these in the Further Reading at the end of this book. However, it is a pleasure to acknowledge here some of those friends and colleagues who over the years have made a more personal contribution to my knowledge of the life and reign of King George III, to thank them for both their generous help and sometimes unwitting assistance – in particular, Peter Barber, John Goldfinch, Clyve Jones, Charlotte Lochhead, Matthew Shaw, Lara Speicher and the late Robert Smith. I have also to thank the Croome Estate Trust for permission to cite a document in its possession. I owe a special debt of gratitude to my wife, Kathleen, who both encouraged the writing of this book and corrected the text. She has also suggested most of the illustrations.

C. W.
Department of Manuscripts, British Library, 2004

Cover illustration:
Allan Ramsay's portrait of
George III in his Coronation
robes, 1762.
www.bridgeman.co.uk

Endpaper illustration:
Part of a speech given to his first
Parliament by George III.
*The British Library, Add. MS 32684,
f.121*

Half-title page illustration:
The 'Copper Horseman' at Windsor,
by Sir Richard Westmacott.
*Guildhall Library, Corporation
of London*

Title-page illustration:
The Grand Procession to St Paul's
on St George's Day 1789.
*Guildhall Library, Corporation
of London*

First published in 2005 by
The British Library
96 Euston Road
London NW1 2DB

Text © 2005 Christopher Wright
Illustrations © The British Library
Board and other named copyright
holders

British Library Cataloguing in
Publication Data
A catalogue record for this book is
available from The British Library

ISBN 0 7123 4893 X

Designed and typeset
by Andrew Barron @ thextension

Family tree by Cedric Knight

Printed in Hong Kong
by South Sea International Press

Contents

FAMILY TREE OF GEORGE III

━━━━━━━━━━━ House of Stuart 1603–1714
━━━━━━━━━━━ House of Hanover 1714–1837

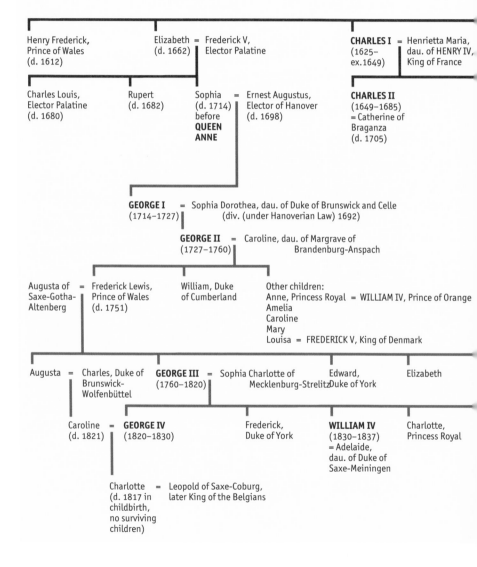

Henry Frederick,
Prince of Wales
(d. 1612)

Elizabeth = Frederick V,
(d. 1662) Elector Palatine

CHARLES I = Henrietta Maria,
(1625–   dau. of HENRY IV,
ex.1649)   King of France

Charles Louis,
Elector Palatine
(d. 1680)

Rupert
(d. 1682)

Sophia   = Ernest Augustus,
(d. 1714) Elector of Hanover
before   (d. 1698)
**QUEEN
ANNE**

CHARLES II
(1649–1685)
= Catherine of
Braganza
(d. 1705)

GEORGE I   = Sophia Dorothea, dau. of Duke of Brunswick and Celle
(1714–1727)   (div. (under Hanoverian Law) 1692)

GEORGE II   = Caroline, dau. of Margrave of
(1727–1760)   Brandenburg-Anspach

Augusta of   = Frederick Lewis,
Saxe-Gotha-   Prince of Wales
Altenberg   (d. 1751)

William, Duke
of Cumberland

Other children:
Anne, Princess Royal = WILLIAM IV, Prince of Orange
Amelia
Caroline
Mary
Louisa = FREDERICK V, King of Denmark

Augusta = Charles, Duke of
          Brunswick-
          Wolfenbüttel

GEORGE III = Sophia Charlotte of
(1760–1820)   Mecklenburg-Strelitz

Edward,
Duke of York

Elizabeth

Caroline = **GEORGE IV**
(d. 1821) (1820–1830)

Frederick,
Duke of York

WILLIAM IV
(1830–1837)
= Adelaide,
dau. of Duke of
Saxe-Meiningen

Charlotte,
Princess Royal

Charlotte   = Leopold of Saxe-Coburg,
(d. 1817 in   later King of the Belgians
childbirth,
no surviving
children)

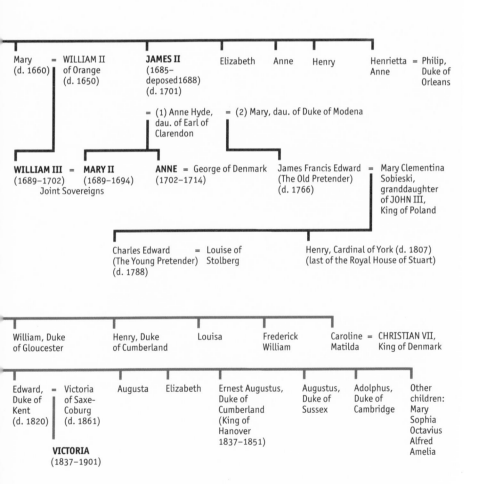

JAMES VI OF SCOTLAND AND I OF ENGLAND
Son of Mary, Queen of Scots
and Henry, Lord Darnley
(1567–1625)
(1603–1625)
= Anne, dau. of
FREDERICK II,
King of Denmark

Mary = WILLIAM II   **JAMES II**   Elizabeth   Anne   Henry   Henrietta = Philip,
(d. 1660) of Orange   (1685–   Anne   Duke of
           (d. 1650)   deposed1688)   Orleans
                       (d. 1701)

= (1) Anne Hyde,   = (2) Mary, dau. of Duke of Modena
  dau. of Earl of
  Clarendon

WILLIAM III = **MARY II**   **ANNE** = George of Denmark   James Francis Edward = Mary Clementina
(1689–1702)   (1689–1694)   (1702–1714)   (The Old Pretender)   Sobieski,
  Joint Sovereigns   (d. 1766)   granddaughter
                                                                                      of JOHN III,
                                                                                      King of Poland

Charles Edward   = Louise of   Henry, Cardinal of York (d. 1807)
(The Young Pretender) Stolberg   (last of the Royal House of Stuart)
(d. 1788)

William, Duke   Henry, Duke   Louisa   Frederick   Caroline = CHRISTIAN VII,
of Gloucester   of Cumberland   William   Matilda   King of Denmark

Edward, = Victoria   Augusta   Elizabeth   Ernest Augustus,   Augustus,   Adolphus,   Other
Duke of   of Saxe-   Duke of   Duke of   Duke of   children:
Kent   Coburg   Cumberland   Sussex   Cambridge   Mary
(d. 1820) (d. 1861)   (King of   Sophia
                                             Hanover   Octavius
                                             1837–1851)   Alfred
                                                                                        Amelia
VICTORIA
(1837–1901)

Introduction

On the morning of 25 October 1760 King George II rose from his bed at Kensington Palace, retired to his closet for the usual purposes and dropped dead. A new reign had begun. The successor to the seventy-six-year-old King was his grandson, George III. The old King had reigned forty-three years. He was an astute politician – relying on the wily Sir Robert Walpole as his Prime Minister until 1742 – and he had presided over an era of prosperity and political stability. He had seen off the last major rebellion on British soil outside Ireland, the Jacobite rising of 1745. He is also famously the last monarch to have commanded his army in person, at Dettingen in 1743, though the fact that this was in Germany underlined his attachment to his German principality, the Electorate of Hanover, to which he made twelve extended visits. However, he was notably lacking in charisma or even charm and few of his subjects mourned him.

Rarely, then, can a monarch have ascended the throne under more propitious circumstances than George III. However, for nearly 150 years after his death, it was the fashion to belittle and denigrate him. He was remembered as the King who lost the American colonies, whose American subjects indeed proclaimed him 'a Tyrant, ... unfit to be the ruler of a free people'. In Britain, where many politicians and scholars adhered to a strongly liberal or 'Whig interpretation of history', which held that the increasing transfer of power from the monarch to Parliament was both an inevitable and desirable development, George III's success in preserving the royal prerogative was seen as an embarrassing anachronism. His opposition, both to the reform of Parliament and the removal of the religious disabilities suffered by Roman Catholics and Protestant nonconformists since the seventeenth century, was ascribed to obstinacy and bigotry. Even his personality was misrepresented. The novelist, William Makepeace Thackeray, who was brought from India to Britain as a

young child, a few years before George III's death, declared: 'Like other dull men, the king was all his life suspicious of superior people ... he was testy at the idea of all innovations, and suspicious of all innovators. He loved mediocrities.' And, of course, on top of everything else, serving as a confirmation of all these judgements, he went mad.

During the last decades of the twentieth century, a more sympathetic view of King George III emerged. A greater understanding of the constitutional position before the passing of the Great Reform Bill of 1832 has made his actions appear less arbitrary. There has been an increasing appreciation that he must be assessed by the political standards of his own age, not another, and a growing awareness that for the majority of his subjects, at least in Britain, he was a much-loved monarch, more popular by far than either his grandfather or his son. Even his terrible illness, which caused him so much anguish and the country so many problems, has begun to yield its secrets to medical historians. It is in the new light cast by these changing perspectives that George III must be judged.

1

A King in waiting
1738–60

The future George III was born on 24 May 1738. After the Gregorian calendar was introduced in Britain in September 1752, subtracting eleven days from that year, his birthday was henceforth celebrated on 4 June. What should have been a joyous event was, in fact, overshadowed by the feud between his parents, the Prince and Princess of Wales, and his grandfather, George II. In any monarchy, there is potential for tension between the reigning sovereign and his heir. Peter the Great of Russia killed his eldest son and Frederick the Great of Prussia, George III's cousin, was forced by his father to watch the beheading of his male lover. In Britain, this strife between the generations was particularly marked in the eighteenth century. Although it may have been exacerbated by family traits, it is also true that successive Hanoverian Princes of Wales were adult for long periods of their predecessors' reigns and the system of parliamentary government in operation presented an irresistible temptation to the heir apparent to ally with the opposition. Just as George II had quarrelled with his father George I, so George III's father, Frederick, Prince of Wales, very quickly quarrelled with his.

Frederick had been born at Hanover in 1707, six years after Parliament, in the 1701 Act of Settlement, had vested the future succession to the English Crown in his great-grandmother, the Electress Sophia, and her descendants. A granddaughter of James I of England and VI of Scotland and a sister of the dashing Prince Rupert, Sophia and her family had been chosen solely because of their religion. Even discounting James II's son, the 'Old Pretender', known by his Jacobite adherents as James III, many had a better claim by birth to the throne. They, however, were Catholics. Sophia, the wife of Ernest Augustus, Duke of Brunswick-Lüneburg and Elector of Hanover, was a Protestant. In 1714, following the death of Queen Anne, the last Stuart to reign in Britain, though the line did not die out until 1807, Sophia's son duly became King George I.

The Protestant Succession was popular; the Hanoverians were not. Frederick was not even brought to Britain from Germany until 1728, the year after his own father had succeeded as George II. He was, in effect, a stranger to his parents and the more they saw of him the less they liked him. George II called Frederick a *wechselbalg*, a changeling, and his mother, Caroline, had, if anything, an even more intense loathing of him. Frederick's marriage in 1736 to Princess Augusta of Saxe-Gotha might have improved matters, but in fact made them worse. When Princess Augusta in due course became pregnant, the King and Queen Caroline decided that she should give birth at Hampton Court, where the Court was in residence, so that they could reassure themselves that their son had not imposed a spurious child on them. To spite his parents, Frederick was equally determined that his first child would not be born under his parents' roof. Accordingly, when in July 1737 her labour pains began and after her waters had broken, his poor wife was hustled into a coach and driven the twelve or so miles to St James's Palace in London, where she was delivered of a little girl also called Augusta. King George II was so outraged by this act of defiance that he ordered the Prince out of the royal palaces. History was repeating itself. George II had been similarly banished by George I. Frederick was eventually to establish himself, as his father had before him, at Leicester House, a property of the Earls of Leicester on the north side of Leicester Square, London. However, his first recourse was to lease the Duke of Norfolk's house in the south-east corner of St James's Square. It was here that in 1738 George III was born. (The building was demolished in 1938, but in its successor on the site a future American President, General Eisenhower, was in 1942 to plan Operation Torch, the allied invasion of North Africa.) Frederick had been made a member of one of the City Livery Companies, the Saddlers. George II's only recorded

TO HER MAJESTY QUEEN CAROLINE
MOST HUMBLE SERVANT. D. M. PAD. 1736

Previous page, left: George III's
mother, Augusta of Saxe-Gotha,
Princess of Wales. Portrait by
Charles Philips, c. 1736.
National Portrait Gallery

Previous page, right: Frederick,
Prince of Wales, eldest son of George II
and father of George III. Portrait by
Philip Mercier, c. 1735–36.
National Portrait Gallery

comment on the continuance of the royal line was the sardonic remark that the saddler's wife had been brought to bed.

The young Prince was two months premature and was not expected to live. That same evening he was baptised George William Frederick, though he received a public baptism on 2 July. His immediate care was entrusted to a wet nurse, Mary Smith, in whose charge he flourished. She was rewarded with the post of royal laundress and her charge, recognizing his very real obligation to her, saw that in due course the post descended to her daughter. In fact, George was fortunate in his immediate circumstances. Given both the constraints of royalty and the customs of the time, Frederick and Augusta were loving parents and took a close interest in their five sons and four daughters. Frederick was widely thought to be a foolish man but his affection for his children is evident in his later letters to them. He was hurt when they neglected to write to him. 'You have a Father who lov's you all tenderly', he told them and assured George, poignantly in view of his own circumstances, that he had 'a Father who (what is not usual) is your best friend'. Whether this friendship would have survived into George's adult life is another question, but Frederick was fated never to see his children grow up. After a brief illness, thought at first to be merely a chill, Frederick died on 20 March 1751. The country was largely unmoved. The anonymous satire 'Here Lies Fred, / Who was alive and is dead; / Had it been his father, / I had much rather' expresses a common view not only of him but also the whole Hanoverian dynasty. Aged only twelve, Prince George was now heir apparent to the throne.

Shortly before his death, Frederick had established his two eldest sons, George and his brother Edward, Duke of York, at Savile House, which adjoined Leicester House. This was to be George's London home until his accession.

The young Prince's household was headed by a Governor with, under him, a Preceptor, who was in charge of his education. Frederick had appointed the Reverend Francis Ayscough, his Clerk of the Closet and brother-in-law of his Private Secretary, to the latter post. A dry pedant, from 1750 Ayscough was largely supplanted by his own deputy George Lewis Scott, a distinguished mathematician. That same year Lord North, father of the future Prime Minister, was appointed the Prince's Governor. This was not an easy position to hold, since while it answered to the Prince of Wales, its occupant also had to be acceptable to the King and his ministers. After Frederick's death the Whig Government seized the chance to replace North with Lord Harcourt but he resigned the following year, having in a fit of pique accused his staff of favouring the Stuarts and their despotic ideas, and was succeeded by Lord Waldegrave. By 1756 Waldegrave had alienated his pupil and effectively been forced to resign. His unhappy experience is important because his *Memoirs*, published in 1821, along with the gossip of Horace Walpole, who claimed that the young Prince was more or less illiterate, have helped establish the picture of George as a backward, somewhat unattractive child, who was not very bright.

The evidence does not bear this out. Though George himself, as an adolescent, confessed to a consciousness of indolence, he was to become one of the most conscientious and hard-working monarchs ever to wear the crown. He was certainly shy, but his upbringing kept him largely isolated from the world at large and Waldegrave's claim that he could be 'sullen and silent' with a tendency to harbour dislikes, a trait which certainly survived into maturity, probably sprang from the same cause. In 1750 Frederick had laid down for North a rigorous programme of instruction for his two eldest sons, spanning the whole day from seven in the morning, when they rose, until ten in the evening, when they were

Previous page: The young Prince of
Wales (later George III) and Edward
Augustus, Duke of York, with their
tutor Francis Ayscough, by Richard
Wilson, c. 1749.
National Portrait Gallery

back in bed. It included social accomplishments such as dancing and fencing,
and it did allow at least an hour for play before dinner at three o'clock in the
afternoon. Otherwise, the Princes were to labour solidly at Latin, maths and
history. On Sunday mornings, Ayscough was to instruct them in religion, or
rather the doctrines of the Church of England, for an hour and a half. Daunting
though this was, this educational regime gave George a better grounding than he
would have received at the time at any of the great public schools to which most
upper-class boys were sent. His earliest surviving letter dates from 1749 when
he wrote to his grandfather, King George II, to thank him for creating him a
Knight of the Garter and could have been written by any boy of his age. His
accompanying letter in German on the same subject to the Hanoverian Minister
in London certainly could not have been.

Deprived of his father, George was necessarily forced to rely for affection
and advice on his mother. The widowed Princess of Wales, Augusta of Saxe-
Gotha, is one of the most misrepresented figures in British history. For much
of her widowhood she had to endure the most obscene disparagement as well
as endless political insult. Even her agonizing death from cancer of the throat
in 1772 was accompanied by howls of joy from the mob. She was blamed at
the time, and subsequently, for what were seen as her son's faults. Her suspected
influence was summed up by the despotic injunction, 'George, be a King!', later
attributed to her without any evidence. Given that she was retiring and played
no role at all in public life, this degree of opprobrium is quite remarkable. It is,
however, explained simply enough. The friend and patron of Lord Bute, she was
the innocent and inadvertent means of his rise to power.

John Stuart, third Earl of Bute, had been made a Lord of his Bedchamber
by Frederick in 1750. By the mid 1750s he had become his widow's chief political

confidant. In 1755 she appointed him personal tutor to her son. For both of them, Bute seems to have filled the void left by Frederick. Inevitably it was said he was Princess Augusta's lover. Had this been the case, he would never have achieved the almost immediate rapport which he established with her son. Well-educated and obviously well-meaning, Bute clearly answered a pressing need for George, becoming overnight less a father figure than a father confessor, not only a tutor but also a spiritual and political guide in an increasingly alarming world. George was soon writing to him as 'my dearest friend', and remarking 'how little any trust can be placed in most men except yourself'. George's misfortune and Bute's tragedy was that he allowed the young Prince to believe this, probably because he believed it himself. While he was encouraging George to write essays which proclaimed 'The pride, the glory of Britain, and the direct end of its constitution is political liberty', Bute was in the long run to display an ignorance of and incapacity for politics which was greatly to embarrass his royal pupil and colour perceptions of his reign.

Though still immature, Prince George was beginning to be of increasing political significance. He had been created Prince of Wales on 20 April 1751, one month after his father's death. Before many years were out, events began to impinge on his most personal interests. By the standards of the day, his grandfather had already outlived the normal span of most men and even he cannot have expected to reign much longer but, in spite or perhaps because of this, George II was busy making plans for his grandson. He had been greatly impressed by his young cousin, Sophia Caroline of Brunswick-Wolfenbüttel, and considered she would make George an excellent wife. That she was the niece of Frederick the Great might also help protect Hanover from Prussia. The Prince, spurred on by his mother and Bute, violently rejected the match. The idea resurfaced in 1759 and met a similar fate. He would not be 'Wolfenbütteled'. Another royal initiative also created friction. In June 1756 the Prince was eighteen, the age at which, by an Act passed after his father's death in 1751, he could rule as king without a regency. The Government proposed that he should live with his brother at St James's Palace, be given an annual income of £40,000 and his own household under Lord Waldegrave as Groom of the Stole. This ancient office, originally with responsibility for the royal close-stool or commode, effectively made its holder the Prince's senior courtier. George reacted with surprising determination, though everyone suspected he had been put up to it. He insisted that he stay at Savile House, next door to his mother. Far less palatable to George II and his ministers, the future George III would settle for nothing less than 'his dear friend' Lord Bute as Groom of the Stole. In the end, they had little alternative but to give way to him on both points.

'It is not easy to express how well bred and reasonable the Prince appears at his Publick Levee every Thursday and on all other occasions ...'

In some ways Bute's influence was probably beneficial. Any prince must of necessity be an actor on a public stage. He has to know how to conduct himself before his subjects and the wider world. One observer was impressed. 'It is not easy to express how well bred and reasonable the Prince always appears at his Publick Levee every Thursday and on all other occasions. The King of France and the Empress of Germany always shew themselves to great advantage, and this young Prince's behaviour is equal that of either of them. He is supposed to know the true State of this Country and to have the best inclinations to do all in his power to make it flourish.' The opinion may, however, have been partisan. The writer, Edward Wortley Montagu, was Bute's father-in-law.

In 1756 Britain had become embroiled in what was subsequently known as the Seven Years War, in which the respective rivalries of Britain and France in America and India and of Prussia and Austria on the Continent once again erupted into open conflict. On this occasion, Britain's former ally Austria was allied with France. Prince George and Bute were firm supporters of the ministry formed by the Duke of Newcastle and Pitt which George II appointed in 1757. William Pitt the elder strongly advocated the colonial rather than the European aspects of the war although, ironically, he soon invested huge resources in the Continental campaign. The war caused a further deterioration in Prince George's relations with his grandfather – 'this old man' as he disrespectfully described him to Bute. In 1759, the year in which George came of age and took his seat in the House of Lords, he requested to be given a military command so that he could actively assist in the struggle. The request was refused, as all such requests by heirs apparent usually are. This led to an another outburst by the Prince at 'the conduct of this old K[ing]'. However, he did not have long to wait. Though it may have seemed an eternity to George, just over a year later his grandfather was dead.

Accession and the search
for a First Minister 1760–70

George III was proclaimed King by Garter King of Arms in London on
26 October 1760, the day following his accession. Like any new monarch, he was
the beneficiary of a great deal of good will and expectation, and this honeymoon
period lasted for a couple of years. His youth and inexperience, which were to
cause him serious problems, seemed, to begin with, a refreshing contrast to his
dreary and unappealing grandfather. Bute's mother-in-law, Lady Mary Wortley
Montagu, wrote to a friend: 'It appears that all his subjects are enamoured of him.
This is a spectacle I never thought to see in England. What a change! If nutmegs
flowered in our fields, I could scarcely be more surprised.'

What was more, unlike the Hanoverian George I and George II, George III
was not a foreigner. The last monarch who could claim this was Queen Anne,
born almost a century before in 1665. In George III's speech to his first
Parliament, which was drafted by Lord Hardwicke, the King himself wrote and
inserted the famous lines, 'Born and educated in this country, I glory in the name
of Britain'. This was printed in the *London Gazette* and thereafter always quoted
as 'I glory in the name of Briton'. In fact, his father Frederick, though with
much less justification, had also played the British card, affecting an interest in
King Arthur and in the Anglo-Saxon kings. In the year of George's birth he had
commissioned from Thomas Arne the masque *Alfred*, which introduced the song
'Rule Britannia'. The pose was, if nothing else, a convenient stick with which to
beat the 'German' Court. However, the effective defeat of the Stuart cause in
1745–46 coupled with the new King's willingness to receive the Tory Party and
its supporters at Court, meant that George III was a monarch who could appeal
to the whole nation. The greatest historian of the age, Edward Gibbon, who
himself came from a staunchly Tory family, observed the general enthusiasm for
'the accession of a British King' and commented with wry amusement on the

SPQB

later complaint of the Whig politician, Edmund Burke, that the loyalty which Tory squires had once directed to the Stuarts they had now transferred to the House of Hanover.

What sort of country had the young Prince inherited? Of his three kingdoms, England, Scotland and Ireland, the population of England, with Wales, was about six million. By 1800 it was to reach eight and a half million and at his death in 1820 it was probably just under twelve million, having doubled since his accession. The population of Ireland, which was about two and a half million in 1760, was to treble to almost seven million during his reign, a figure which tragically proved unsustainable in the nineteenth century. Scotland was the least populous of his realms. Its population of 1,300,000 in 1760 was probably about two million at his death. London, his capital city, boasted, if its suburbs are included, a population on his accession of about 700,000. This had doubled by

1820. Even after industrialization led to extensive urban growth in the north, London dwarfed all other towns and like every capital was the centre of both government and fashion. Paradoxically though, despite its disproportionate size, it did not dominate national life as was the case of capitals abroad. The British ruling classes remained essentially rural both in their outlook and their image of themselves. This was largely because, as a consequence of the constitutional upheavals of the previous century culminating in the Glorious Revolution of 1688 which drove the despotic James II from the throne, the monarch had to share power with the landed gentry, of which the nobility formed merely the topmost layer.

Though the government was the King's, in reality he shared power with Parliament. Only this could vote the taxes which allowed the administration to function. Of Parliament's two Houses, Lords and Commons, the Commons had to be elected at least every seven years and in 1760 had 558 members, representing the counties and boroughs of England, Scotland and Wales. Ireland had its own Parliament. Though the qualification for voting differed from seat to seat and was held by only a small proportion of the population, most significant male property holders were represented and even many who did not have the vote felt involved in the political process. Britain, like almost all European countries of the day, was a 'confessional' state, with a prescribed form of religious observance. Those who did not belong to the state church were seen as a threat and their rights were limited. In England every holder of a government office had to belong to the Church of England, but this was a broad church and Protestant dissenters flourished. Taken together, its relative tolerance of political and religious diversity meant that Britain was out of step with most other European monarchies, something recognized both in Britain and abroad.

The political and intellectual liberty
that existed in the country was
unparalleled in the other major states
and its inhabitants prided themselves
on being both British and free.

The political and intellectual liberty that existed in the country was unparalleled in the other major states and its inhabitants prided themselves on being both British and free. These were restraints on royal power of which the young Prince was well aware. Indeed, one of his schoolboy essays remarked 'let us still remember we stand in debt for our liberty and religion to the success of 1688'.

The new King was the focus of all eyes. A monarch may or may not be of political significance – George III had less than most of his Continental cousins though much more than his modern descendants – but he must always be the personification of the nation. The nature of monarchy means that the constitution of the state will be viewed not as a legalistic social contract, devoid of warmth and humanity, but as a relationship between individuals. For the monarch it is the difference between being the head of a big corporation and the head of an extended family. Not just the official actions but the personality and family life of the sovereign are of intense concern to his subjects, just as those of a father or mother would be.

What struck his subjects about their new ruler was not only that he was young and personable but also that he was unmarried. The year before his accession he had fallen in love with Lady Sarah Lennox. She was a great-granddaughter of Charles II but, unfortunately, also the sister-in-law of Henry Fox, widely viewed as the most rapacious and unscrupulous politician of the age. In no sense would it have been a politic match. After he became King, George began a discreet search for a bride amongst the Protestant princesses of Europe. Most were disqualified by defects of birth or temperament. His eventual choice was the exceedingly obscure Charlotte of Mecklenburg-Strelitz, a small duchy just south of Germany's Baltic coast. Arranged marriages were still largely the norm amongst the upper classes of society, where family alliances and the inheritance of land remained predominating factors, though royalty alone had rarely met their intended partners before. Surprisingly, some of these marriages worked well. That of George and Charlotte, in particular, was to be a conspicuous success.

The marriage negotiations were carried out in great secrecy in the early summer of 1761. They were hastened by George's desire that he should have his bride by his side at his Coronation, which was to take place on 22 September 1761. The young Princess Charlotte – she was only seventeen – arrived at Harwich on 7 September, after a week and a half at sea, and reached London the next day. George and Charlotte were married that evening at the Chapel Royal, St James's Palace, by Matthew Sutton, Archbishop of Canterbury. A fortnight later they were crowned together at Westminster Abbey by the Archbishop. During the ceremony George was anointed with holy oil. This act of consecration, referring back to the Old Testament, was the most sacred part of the ritual and the performance of Handel's anthem to the text 'Zadok the priest and Nathan the prophet anointed Solomon King', composed for the coronation of George's grandfather, pointed up the significance of the moment. However, the King was also required to take an oath to defend the Protestant constitution, and George's rigid adherence to this oath was to become of major importance in the latter part of his reign.

The King and Queen processed from Westminster Hall to the Abbey and back again on a raised walkway. All the houses with a view of the scene were fronted with temporary boxes made from scaffolding and hung with carpets and cloths, and the lucky householders charged huge sums for admission to these structures. The ceremony ended with a grand banquet in the mediaeval splendour of Westminster Hall. At this, by tradition, the King's Champion rode in to throw

Enamel plaques of King George and
Queen Charlotte, by William Hopkins
Craft, 1773.
British Museum

down the gauntlet to anyone who challenged the King's title. Lord Talbot, the Lord Steward, excited great applause by succeeding in making his horse walk backwards, so that he did not have to turn his face from the monarch. Coronation banquets were invariably somewhat chaotic affairs. The spectators in the galleries lowered baskets for any friends and well-wishers amongst the diners to fill with food for them. At the end, after the guests had departed, the public were admitted and allowed to make off not only with any food that was left but also with all the remaining fittings. There was some demand that the event be made more accessible to the general public. Samuel Johnson, the future compiler of the first modern dictionary, provided the text for a pamphlet which argued for an extended route for the procession. George was certainly conscious of the value of public ceremonial. Shortly after his Coronation he ordered the new Gold State Coach, first seen when he opened Parliament in November 1762, and now regularly used by monarchs at their Coronations.

The King's marriage and Coronation set the seal on the new reign. At the personal and domestic level this flourished. The Queen was soon accepted by her new country. In her honour, London was to boast a Mecklenburgh Square, English kitchens created the Apple Charlotte and the world of botany named the striking southern African bloom the *Strelitzia*. The marriage itself was fruitful. A son and heir, the future George IV, was born on 12 August 1762 and created Prince of Wales a week later. Eight more sons and six daughters followed at almost yearly intervals until the last, Princess Amelia, was born in 1783. On the public and political front, however, the first decade of the King's reign was markedly less successful. He was in search of an agreeable and durable Prime Minister. He was not to find one until 1770.

On his accession, the political turmoil of the 1760s might not have been predicted. George III had come to the throne in the middle of a hugely successful war. In Canada General James Wolfe had destroyed France's ambitions in North America, while in Asia Robert Clive's victories had ensured that Britain not France would be the dominant European power in India. George, however, suffered from two major drawbacks. One fed on the other. He was inexperienced and naïve. The young King was genuinely religious and he took private and public morality very seriously. Almost his first official act after his accession was to issue a proclamation 'for the encouragement of piety and virtue, and for the preventing and punishing of vice, profaneness, and immorality'. If eighteenth-century Britain is viewed through the satirical canvases of William Hogarth, this may seem a vain gesture, but even Hogarth's art was an argument for the triumph of virtue over vice. In the country at large religious revivals, such as Methodism, were taking hold. In the long term George III's moral seriousness was to serve him well. It echoed a changing mood amongst increasing numbers of his subjects.

However, George's idealism also extended to politics. This has been attributed to various causes, some of them malign. A poem published on his accession admonished him:

Proceed, great Prince, a Patriot King compleat,
And *George* the *Third* henceforth be *George* the *Great*.

These innocent words possibly hinted at the supposed influence of Lord Bolingbroke's political essay, *The Idea of a Patriot King*, which had been dedicated to George's father, Frederick. Many contemporaries took a jaundiced view of this work. Since Bolingbroke was a Tory and a Jacobite, as the followers of the Stuart King James II and his Catholic descendants were called, it followed that his work must be a conduit of Stuart despotism. Bolingbroke was a very clever man but a wildly impractical politician who enjoyed the distinction of having been dismissed their service by both George I and the Old Pretender. At one level his book was a justification of Frederick, Prince of Wales, leading the opposition to his father's ministers. In reality, though, it was a utopian tract. Its philosophical justification was the fallacy, now more common on the left than the right of politics, that all good men must necessarily take the same view. If they do not, they are not only mistaken but also almost certainly corrupt, if not financially, then morally. In fact, this fitted well with the common eighteenth-century view that political parties as such were bad, expressions of faction and personal ambition.

This was certainly the opinion of King George as it was of his tutor Bute. George III wanted all good men to put faction behind them and to serve the nation. This may have been a political programme, albeit an unworldly one. What it was not was a political philosophy. George believed in the division of powers between King, Lords and Commons and he only sought to increase the power of the Crown in so far as he thought it had been improperly encroached on. Unfortunately, this belief left him ill-equipped to deal with the reality of the political world. His chief political ambition, as it had been that of his predecessors, was to avoid what was picturesquely known as 'storming the Closet', the imposition on him by political factions of a minister he did not want.

In most European states the king's favourite was also his first minister. In Britain the situation was more complicated. When George II came to the throne he had intended to replace his father's minister Sir Robert Walpole with his own favourite, Spencer Compton, Lord Wilmington, but Wilmington proved incapable even of drafting the King's Accession Speech to the Privy Council. The First, or

Throughout his life no one was to
be more resolute than George III
in supporting the use of force to
combat what he saw as aggression,
but by inclination he was pacific.
He saw war as a reckless
squandering of lives and money.

Prime, Minister had to carry on the monarch's business, above all in Parliament. George II had fallen back on Walpole. Few people doubted that his grandson intended to vest power in Bute. In fact, Bute had little political experience and would have been happy to be the power behind the throne if this had been an option. Even if George III had been prepared to countenance it, Bute's rivals for office certainly were not.

The Prime Minister whom the new King inherited, the elderly Duke of Newcastle, embodied everything about eighteenth-century politics that George despised. He saw Newcastle as corrupt, which, at a personal level, was unfair. A lifetime of political office left the Duke poorer than when he started. He was, though, a master of oiling the wheels of government by the judicious use of patronage – the offer of a place here, an honour there – what George called 'these dirty arts'. The real power in the ministry was William Pitt, one of the two Secretaries of State, and the driving force behind an aggressive war policy. Both George and Bute wanted peace with France, partly because they thought, rightly, that Britain had already made spectacular military gains but also, to some extent, on moral grounds. Throughout his life no one was to be more resolute than George III in supporting the use of force to combat what he saw as aggression, but by inclination he was pacific. He saw war as a reckless squandering of lives and money.

The drive for peace with France brought about the resignation first of Pitt, in 1761, and then, the following year, of Newcastle. The way was now clear to fulfil George's dearest wish. On 26 May 1762 Bute became Prime Minister. The favourite was in two minds before accepting. The chief criticism that can be voiced against him is that he lacked the strength of character to refuse. It was a post which he earnestly desired and one for which he knew he was profoundly

The Rape of the Petti-coat.

He valiantly seiz'd the Petti-coat and Boot at the Portal of his own Mansion.

Daily adv.

unsuited. He is that saddest of figures, one whose ambition outruns his talent.
The chief requirement of high office is the hide of a rhinoceros. Bute was fatally
thin-skinned. Unlike the King, who endured the attacks of the London poor and
even assassination attempts apparently unflinching, Bute shrank from the tumult
of public life. And for a timid man, there was much to fear. The mob pulled his
carriage to pieces and pilloried his supposed relationship with the King's mother.
Parliament was just as alarming. On Bute fell the burden of securing its consent
to the Treaty of Paris and all manner of trivial but contentious legislation. Since
he was in the Lords, he needed someone to oversee the Government's business
in the Commons and saw no option but to rely on Henry Fox. Fox, as Paymaster
General, had made a business out of public administration. Though this was quite
legal, even contemporaries thought he overdid it. George was horrified but was
prepared to pay the price if it would help Bute. He was, therefore, taken aback
when almost immediately Bute began to hint at resignation. Their mission,
George wrote to him, had been 'purging out corruption'. Bute's departure would
leave the Ministry composed 'of the most abandoned men that ever held those
offices'. It was, however, only a matter of time.

By April 1763 Bute had had enough and suggested Fox as his successor.
Fox declined and Bute then alighted on George Grenville, one of the Secretaries
of State. Grenville was intended to be a front man. Bute would continue as
favourite while the new Prime Minister coped with the stresses and strains of
office. Only someone as naïve as Bute could have thought this would work.
He was soon frozen out. In later years George was to wonder how he could
ever have placed any reliance in the man he had called 'my dearest friend'.
However, Bute still cast a heavy shadow. The understandable but, as it turned
out, completely unnecessary fear of his secret influence poisoned Grenville's

Opposite: John Wilkes had the
support of the London mob against
the King, and incited rioting and
civil unrest during the 1760s.
Portrait by Robert Pine, c. 1768.
www.bridgeman.co.uk

relationship with the King. Meanwhile, Grenville had to cope with the legacy
of Bute's unpopularity as represented by the person of John Wilkes.

What seems important to contemporaries and what with hindsight turns
out to have real significance are often very different things. No better illustration
of this can be found than the first decade of the reign of George III. Grenville's
Stamp Act of 1765 to raise taxes from the American colonies went relatively
unnoticed in Britain despite the momentous consequences that were to flow
from it. What occupied both Government and public was not fear of revolution
in America but of upheaval at home, a fear embodied by Wilkes. In fact, Wilkes
was little more than an unlicensed 'Lord of Misrule'. His scurrilous paper the
North Briton was in its very title a satire on the Scottish Lord Bute, and the
notorious issue 45, dated St George's Day, 1763, claimed that the King's Speech
to Parliament contained a lie in asserting that the Peace of Paris, which ended
Britain's involvement in the Seven Years War, had led to a general European
peace. The ministers had Wilkes sent to the Tower of London but the rights he
enjoyed as a Member of Parliament secured his release. The London mob rioted
in his support, burning a boot and a petticoat in ungallant reference to the King's
favourite and his mother. By the end of the year Wilkes had fled to the
Continent and Grenville had him expelled from Parliament. In 1768 he returned
and was elected M.P. for Middlesex, was expelled again, and re-elected three
times though the election was awarded to his opponent, before finally being
readmitted to Parliament in 1774. The London mob again rioted in his favour
with the resonant cry of 'Wilkes and Liberty'. Liberty had little to do with it.
For the people, spurred on by economic distress, it was a God-given opportunity
to make fun of authority. George III much approved of the steps taken against
Wilkes, not least because of his horror at the man's open immorality. A member

'John Wilkes's, Esq; and Liberty', a song
praising Wilkes and attacking Bute,
from *The Scots Scourge: or Pridden's
Supplement to the British Antidote to
Caledonian Poison* (1765), vol 2, p.47.
The British Library, 1422.b.18

of the Hell Fire Club, Wilkes had published the obscene *Essay on Woman*. In the
event, this turmoil signified very little. Wilkes himself was to end up a steadfast
political supporter of the King.

While this sideshow rumbled on, politics itself became little more than an
elaborate game of musical chairs amongst the political class. The King was
determined not 'to yield to faction' but faction was all there was. Grenville soon

made himself hateful to the King. Just as George's granddaughter Victoria was later to find Gladstone tiresome because he addressed her as he would a public meeting, George III had to submit to interminable and disobliging lectures from his First Minister. By 1765 George was looking to replace Grenville with Newcastle and Pitt. Grenville found out and overreacted. Quite incorrectly, he blamed Bute, forced the King to dismiss Bute's remaining supporters and yield up almost all royal patronage. George was humiliated. He turned to his uncle the Duke of Cumberland, who cobbled together a ministry under Lord Rockingham. Rockingham was to be revered by later generations as a leader of the Whigs but he proved an incompetent First Minister. By July 1766 the King had fallen back on William Pitt, the 'Great Commoner', now created Earl of Chatham. With some justice George must have hoped that this time he had really secured a stable and long-lasting ministry.

The King had reckoned without Pitt's mercurial temperament and ill-health. In December Pitt retreated to Bath with gout. At George's urgent request he returned to London in March 1767 but, though he remained nominal Prime Minister until October 1768, was too unwell to play any further part in Government. Responsibility for this fell on the Duke of Grafton, who in due course succeeded to the office, as he had already to the duties of Pitt. However, the moment he had surrendered the seals of office Pitt began to recover and soon went into opposition to his successor. By January 1770 Grafton, too, considered he had suffered enough. He resigned. On 28 January Lord North, the Chancellor of the Exchequer and Leader of the Commons as well as being the son of the King's former Governor, was appointed Prime Minister. The years of ministerial confusion were over. George III thought that at last he had found the Prime Minister for whom he was searching.

3   British settlement on the North
American coast had begun in Virginia
in the early seventeenth century, and
gathered speed after the Restoration ...

The American War 1770–82

In 1770 George III and his new Prime Minister, Lord North, both looked forward to an era of peace and stability. In many ways their wishes were fulfilled. In the decade since George's accession there had been six Prime Ministers and an air of continuous political crisis. North was to remain in office until 1782. In the eighteenth century this record was surpassed only by Sir Robert Walpole, Prime Minister from 1721 to 1742. However, this stability was to come under increasing threat. Both men were to be overwhelmed by a crisis which neither had sought but which was to weaken their grasp on power and has damaged their reputations ever since – the loss of the American colonies.

British settlement on the North American coast had begun in Virginia in the early seventeenth century, and gathered speed after the Restoration, not least with the capture of New York from the Dutch in 1664. By the time Georgia was established in 1732, there were thirteen colonies, all with different constitutions and with no formal links with one another. The colonies were surrounded by a hostile indigenous population and, potentially more dangerous, by the French, long established in Canada in the north and in Louisiana to the west where they were thrusting up the course of the Mississippi from New Orleans. Together with their native allies they seemed to pose a significant threat. George III had in his library a manuscript copy of the diary of Lt Robert Orme, which described the defeat and death of General Braddock in 1755 at the hands of the Indians while leading a force to attack the French at Fort Duquesne, the modern Pittsburg. On a single page of this journal, as members of Braddock's force, occur two names that were to be heard again, Thomas Gage and George Washington. What was to happen in the next twenty years that was to pit such men against one another?

One cause was British success in the Seven Years War of 1756–63. French power was obliterated. All that remained of France's vast empire in North

America were the tiny islands of St Pierre and Miquelon, off the southern
coast of Newfoundland. Canada was ceded to Britain and Louisiana to Spain.
However, the war had been immensely costly and in the new era of financial
prudence and economy which prevailed at Westminster, British politicians again
asked themselves how the expense of administering and defending the American
colonies might be defrayed. George Grenville's answer was to extend the duty
on a wide range of legal and commercial documents that applied in Britain to
America. Shortly after the Stamp Act became law, Grenville fell from power.
It was his hapless successor Rockingham who had to cope with the civil
commotion and downright intimidation of government officials that swept
America. Some of the radicals such as the 'Sons of Liberty' at New York even
invoked the name of John Wilkes in their cause. Here was someone they could
identify with, who like them, as they saw it, had stood up to an overweening
executive. The colonists objected not only to the tax, they said, but also to
the principle. They had not voted for these taxes and the cry was raised of
'No Taxation without Representation'. This was not the only source of dispute
between the mother country and the colonists – they also objected to the lands
west of the Allegheny Mountains being reserved for the native population –
but it was the chief bone of contention.

It was not, however, the only principle at stake. Its converse was that the
Westminster Parliament – or as constitutional doctrine expressed it, the Crown
in Parliament – saw itself as exercising sovereign power throughout the British
Empire. Though Rockingham repealed the Stamp Act as unenforceable, the
notion that Parliament could not legislate for British subjects anywhere seemed
intolerable. The Americans might not be directly represented in Parliament but,
then, neither were most Britons, few of whom had the vote. The ministers

Proofs stamps issued under the Stamp
Duty Act to enable Britain to charge
duty on newspapers and legal and
commercial documents in America.
*The British Library, Philatelic Section,
Inland Revenue Archives, List 6, Bk 3, 35*

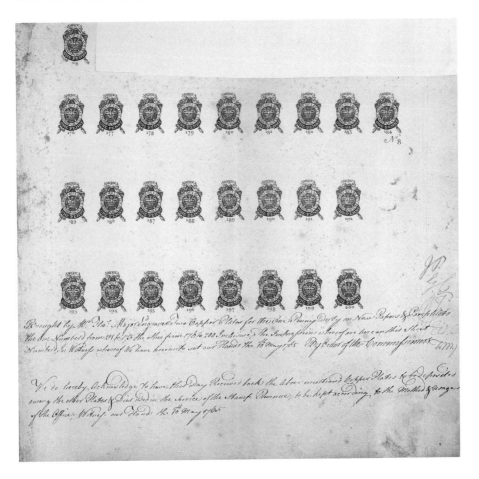

Opposite: Cantonment of His Majesty's
Forces in North America, 1766,
showing the boundaries of British
territory and the extent of the lands
reserved for the Indians.
The British Library, Add. MS 11288

pressed on, passing the Declaratory Act of 1766 – 'An act for better securing
the dependency of his majesty's dominions in America upon the crown and
parliament of Great Britain'. In 1767, specifically to defray the cost of
administering America, Charles Townshend, the Chancellor of the Exchequer,
imposed duties in America on glass, lead, paper and tea and set up Commissioners
of Customs and Excise to administer them. The legislative powers of the fractious
New York Assembly were also suspended. At this point Townshend died, leaving
others to administer an intensely unpopular system. One of North's first acts as
Prime Minister was to repeal these duties, though he chose to leave them in
place on tea, at three pence per pound, to uphold the principle. Unfortunately
the situation was inflamed by a measure intended to assist the failing East India
Company. In 1773 it was given the right to export duty-free tea to America,
which would have allowed it to undercut the price of the tea which American
merchants were smuggling in. The first consignment to arrive at Boston was duly
dumped in the harbour on 16 December 1773 by a large crowd disguised as
Indians. This was the famous 'Boston Tea Party'. From then on it was down hill
all the way.

What was the role of George III in all of this? Like most others he
accepted, without question, the principle of the sovereignty of Parliament
in America. He had initiated none of the unpopular legislation but, as a
constitutional monarch, he saw it as his duty to support his ministers. The
discontent in America would have seemed little different from that which he
had observed at home. Customs duties were unpopular in Britain and there was
regular violence, in some cases almost pitched battles, between customs officers
and smugglers. Merchants were often opposed to government. This was certainly
true in his own capital in the first part of his reign. In 1774 Wilkes was actually

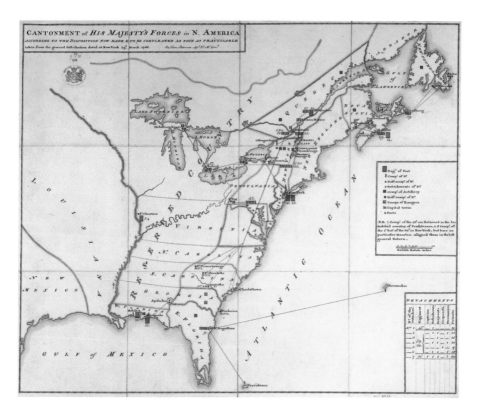

elected Lord Mayor of London, and strongly supported the Americans. Riots and civil disturbance were frequent and, since there was no proper police force to contain them, the use of troops often led to bloodshed. Against this background, the Boston Massacre of 1770, in which troops killed five protesters against customs duties, would have seemed regrettable but little out of the ordinary.

Though George would have realized that American society was different from that in Britain – he did, after all, everything he could to bolster the Church of England there – he probably had little sense of how very different it was; that it was still a frontier society, which had not yet evolved the forms and usages that a thousand years of history had made an integral part of life at home and which rendered English society in particular so cohesive. Some, indeed, had gone to America specifically to escape the restraints of that cohesion, the Quakers in Pennsylvania, for example, and other religious radicals. This meant that in America the populace was even more volatile than at home and far less supportive of Government. Even amongst the loyalists of Canada, Governor

Thomas Parr observed in 1786: 'it's the natural Disposition of People on this side the Atlantic, to kick against the King's Governors; I have seen a good deal of it, as well as a natural levelling principle which they inherit by Instinct.'

Finally, the King seems to have had no sense that what his Government was up against, across the North Atlantic, was a burgeoning nationalism. Indeed, he would have had no word to express the idea since it did not come into common use until the nineteenth century. Consequently, it is not surprising that he adopted the same attitude towards the American disturbances as he did to those in Britain – that he must try to be fair, but that above all he must be firm. This sentiment would have been strengthened because it was the advice the Government was receiving from many of its servants in America, but the King would have held it in any case. Being fair but firm characterized all George's actions. It was a trait which can be seen clearly during the anti-Catholic Gordon Riots of 1780 when, for almost a week, London was in the hands of the mob and only the King kept his head. He knew that to show weakness could lead only to anarchy. It was a firmness, though, which Americans were to hold against him.

Across the ocean, the situation slipped inexorably out of control. The attempt to restore order by besieging Boston and installing Gage as Governor of Massachusetts proved a political and military disaster. It inspired the meeting of the first Continental Congress of most of the states at Philadelphia in September and October 1774. On 11 September the King wrote to North, 'the die is now cast, the colonies must either submit or triumph'. By 18 November George could not disguise from himself that 'the New England Governments are in a state of rebellion, blows must decide whether they are to be subject to this country or independent'. Given this analysis, Gage's failure to overawe the malcontents militarily proved decisive. With a frustration that all public servants will recognize,

Part of a letter to Lord Barrington, Secretary at War, from the Governor of Massachusetts General Gage, in 1775, pleading for more support in the colonies.
The British Library, Add. MS 73550, f. 76v

Massachusetts Delegates have had too great an Influence amongst them. It's now neither this Point nor the other but affairs are general, they are your subjects or not. This Province and the Neighbouring ones, particularly Connecticut, are preparing for war; If you will resist and not yield, that Resistance should be effectual at the Beginning. If you think ten Thousand Men sufficient, send Twenty, if one Million is thought enough, give two; you will save both Blood and Treasure in the End. A large Force will terrify and engage many to join you, a middling one will encourage Resistance, and gain no Friends. The Crisis is indeed an alarming one, and Britain had never more need of wisdom, firmness and union than at this Juncture. I sincerely wish a happy End to these Broils and am with all Respect and Regard,

My Lord,
your Lordship's
most obedient,
and most humble servant,

Tho: Gage.

345

1775

By The King,

A Proclamation for suppressing Rebellion and Sedition.

G. R.

Whereas many of Our Subjects in divers parts of Our Colonies and plantations in North America, misled by the Instigation of dangerous and ill designing Men, and forgetting the Duty they owe to the Power that has protected and sustained them, ~~have~~, after various illegal & disorderly Acts, proceeded ~~at length~~ to an open and avowed Rebellion, by a levying war against Us, Their Crown & Dignity, and whereas +

committed in disturbance of the publick Peace have at length

arraying themselves in warlike manner to withstand the execution of the Law &

~~and~~ there is reason to apprehend that such rebellion

To the End that none of our Subjects may neglect or violate their duty thro' ignorance thereof or of the protection which the Law will afford to their Loyalty & Zeal

~~We have therefore thought~~ fit, for the better and ~~more speedy suppressing~~

50

Die Zerstörung der Königlichen Bild | La Destruction de la Statue roye
Säule zu Neu Yorck | a Nouvelle Yorck

Gage pleaded with the British Government for more support. 'This Province and
the neighbouring ones, particularly Connecticut, are preparing for war; If you
will resist and not yield, that Resistance should be effectual at the Beginning.
If you think ten Thousand men sufficient, send Twenty, if one million is thought
enough, give two; you will save both Blood and Treasure in the End.' He received
no troops, only instructions to do something.

Deciding on seizing the stores of the local militia, he sent out a detachment
of troops. On 19 April 1775, in a brief skirmish at Lexington and a bloodier

encounter at Concord, the first shots of the American War of Independence were fired. Gage himself was soon besieged in Boston. The Second Continental Congress agreed to raise troops and appointed Washington Commander-in-Chief of the Army of the United Colonies. At the same time it sent 'The Olive Branch Petition' to London calling for the return of the previous 'mild and just government' and asking the King 'to direct some mode by which the united applications of your faithful colonists ... may be improved into a happy and permanent reconciliation'. The King thought the petition disingenuous and refused to receive it as it would have admitted the legality of the Continental Congress. On 23 August 1775 a royal proclamation declared the colonies to be in a state of rebellion, which they undoubtedly were. On 4 July 1776 Congress formally declared its independence. Five days later the statue of George III on the Bowling Green at New York was pulled down.

The personal nature of the venom directed against the King might appear surprising. In the Declaration of Independence twenty-five lines are spent denouncing him, only four in complaining at the British in general. 'The history of the present King of Great Britain is a history of repeated injuries and usurpations, all having in direct object the establishment of an absolute Tyranny over these States ... A Prince, whose character is thus marked by every act which may define a Tyrant, is unfit to be the ruler of a free people.' As a description of George III this is a grotesque parody. It was not intended to be an accurate portrait but potent propaganda. What is striking is that there is no mention at all of the British Government. All its acts were, of course, carried out in the King's name. George III, like any monarch, was the personification of the state. In fact, it was the British state that the colonial radicals were in revolt against but it was the person of the King that they pilloried.

'It is now understood, on all hands,
that the continuation of the
American war was owing to the
personal stubbornness of the king.'

The date, too, of this vilification may be remarked. It was at the beginning
of the conflict, whereas it is George III's conduct after 1776 that is most open to
question. Ironically, if there is a real criticism of the King it is not that he
precipitated the war but that he prolonged it once it had started. The essayist
Leigh Hunt, whose parents were American Tories, persecuted and driven out of
Philadelphia by the radicals, could write in the mid-nineteenth century as if it
were a commonplace: 'It is now understood, on all hands, that the continuation
of the American war was owing to the personal stubbornness of the king.'
Indeed, Hunt's mother came to think that George III's later insanity was a
judgement of providence for causing so much unnecessary bloodshed. The King's
justification was that if the rebels were to be opposed by force, and most British
opinion insisted that they should be, then at least this policy should be carried
out as with as much determination as possible.

Lord North had many virtues, but he was not a resolute war minister and
things soon started to go badly. On 17 October 1777 Burgoyne, who was leading
a British force from Canada, was surrounded and forced to surrender at Saratoga.
This inspired the French and later the Dutch and Spanish to enter the war on the
American side. In 1778 North told the King that he wished to resign. George III
persuaded him to do no such thing. He had begun his reign as a believer in the
virtues of peace and opposed to an aggressive foreign policy. However, once the
conflict had started he saw no alternative but to see it through. 'If others will not
be active,' he was to declare to Sandwich, 'I must drive.'

Even now the King deferred to his ministers. He himself had come round
to a defensive military policy, placing reliance on the fleet. The Cabinet, however,
insisted on sending more troops. This was easier said than done. Unlike most
European states Britain did not have a large standing army. It had already had to

A New Map of HUDSON'S BAY and LABRADOR from a late Survey of the Coasts of Hudson's Bay.

HUDSON'S BAY

NEW NORTH WALES

SOUTH WALES

LABRADOR or NEW BRITAIN

NEW F

LAKE SUPERIOR

LAKE HU

LAKEH

EASTERN SIOUX

SIOUX OR NADOUESSIANS

WESTERN SIOUX

OUTOUAIS OUTAWA

OUTAGAMIS

MASCOUTENS

COUNTRY OF THE ADOUCAS

PANIS

OSAGES

VIRGI

OHIO

NORTH CARO

CHEROKEES

ARANSAS

CHICASAWS

SOUTH CAROLI

CREEK INDIANS

LOUISIANA

CHACTAWS

GEORGIA

COUNTRY OF THE CENIS

COUNTRY OF THE PALACHEES

TIMOOQUAS

FLORIDA

Previous page: The Red-lined Map of
1782, showing the proposed boundaries
of the newly independent United
States, together with the surviving
British territories in North America.
The British Library, K. Top. CXVIII, 49.b

rely on the German, particularly Hessian, mercenaries, which the King had been able to hire on the Continent. Whatever their military value, these much-hated soldiers proved a political liability in the colonies. In consequence, more of Britain's scarce military resources had to be sent to America just when a European war threatened. It was all, of course, to no avail. Lord Cornwallis, the future Governor General of India, was besieged in Yorktown, Virginia. On 19 October 1781, he surrendered. Everything George III had striven so gallantly to avoid now came to pass.

What had made the King so determined in his course of action? In part, he reflected the views of a large part of the nation. The actions of the rebellious colonists' leaders had caused great indignation in Britain and, until the beginning of 1782, there was a majority in Parliament for the military campaign against them. No one expected the catastrophic reverses that occurred. The colonists themselves were scarcely united in their views. There were innumerable loyalists throughout the colonies who were appalled at what the 'Patriots' were doing. Many suffered terribly at the hands of these enthusiasts and a large number were either driven out or chose to leave, returning to Britain or moving to Canada. Flora Macdonald, who had suffered imprisonment in the Tower of London for helping the Stuart Young Pretender 'Bonnie Prince Charlie' to escape after the Battle of Culloden in 1746, now endured exile from North Carolina for her loyalty to a Hanoverian King. Thirty thousand people moved to Nova Scotia alone. A new colony, Upper Canada, was peopled by the townships these loyalists founded. In terms of the proportion of the population affected, it was one of the great forced migrations of history. Above all, for the King – and here, from the opposite standpoint, even John Wilkes agreed with him – the separation of America from the mother country would mean the end of the British Empire and the reduction of Britain to a minor European state. In a letter of 11 June 1779 to North, George spelt out the logic of this: if America became independent, the West Indies would follow and become dependent on it. Ireland would quickly go down the same path. British trade would be annihilated 'and soon [we] would be a poor island indeed'.

In the event, many of these fears were to prove unfounded. The Preliminary Articles of Peace were signed at Paris between Britain and the colonists on 30 November 1782 and at Versailles between Britain, France and Spain on 20 January 1783. The definitive treaties were both signed on 3 September. An official copy of the boundaries of the new state with his surviving territories in North America, the famous Red-lined Map, was prepared for the King. Alas, peace did not lead to amity. The King's own bitterness found vivid expression. 'Knavery,' he wrote of his former dominion, 'seems to be so much the striking feature of its Inhabitants that it may not in the end be an evil they become Aliens to this Kingdom.' When John Adams arrived in 1785 as the first American envoy to his Court, George III received him graciously. 'I was the last to consent to the separation; but the separation having been made and having become inevitable, I have always said, as I say now, that I would be the first to meet the friendship of the United States as an independent power.' His true feelings can only be imagined. The war had hardened already entrenched attitudes on both sides. Dislike and distrust characterized Anglo-American relations for well over a century. Though George III was probably unaware of the fact, before his death there was, between 1812 and 1815, to be another war between the mother country and her turbulent offspring. The foundation myth of the United States required that, however unfairly, the King be cast as a villain. The new nation found its personification in another George, George Washington.

4

The King's position re-established 1782–1810

To observers at the time the American War appeared fatally to have undermined the King's position. George III himself certainly thought so. He seriously considered abdication though he did not despair for long, difficult as the situation was. The war had invigorated the opposition and given them an issue on which to campaign. Insultingly, the British Whigs, the supporters of the revolutionary settlement of 1688, adopted for their election rosettes the colours worn by Washington's troops, buff and blue. In due course these colours were to be taken up by the most famous of Whig publications, the Scottish quarterly, the *Edinburgh Review*, founded in 1802. Meanwhile, the strains in the body politic were manifesting themselves in other ways. The Reverend Christopher Wyvill was active in drafting the 1780 Yorkshire petition for the reform of Parliament. Edmund Burke advocated an Economical Reform Bill for cutting the costs of government and John Dunning, who sat for Lord Shelburne's borough at Calne in Wiltshire, carried his famous motion that 'the influence of the Crown has increased, is increasing, and ought to be diminished'. On top of all this, the defeat of the British army at Yorktown, Virginia, in 1781 led directly to the fall of the Government in Britain the following spring. 'At last the fatal day is come,' as the King observed. On 20 March 1782, after twelve years in office, Lord North announced his resignation to the Commons.

   Whoever succeeded him would be faced with negotiating the peace with the victorious Americans. The King wished to appoint Shelburne, the 'Jesuit in Berkeley Square' as he had disparagingly called him only a few years before. Shelburne declined to head the new administration, fearing the strength of Rockingham and his supporters. George III took an even dimmer view of Rockingham than he did of Shelburne but authorized the latter to negotiate with him. On 27 March Rockingham was appointed Prime Minister. Shelburne

Previous page: George III in middle
age, a portrait initial from a grant of
nobility, 1797.
The British Library, Add. MS 30276

and Charles James Fox, the son of Henry Fox, became Secretaries of State.
None of the old Cabinet was included. This was to be a reformed and reforming
ministry. Many well-paid posts whose duties had long disappeared were to be
abolished. The Irish Parliament was granted legislative autonomy. The old
Northern and Southern Departments were reshaped as the Foreign Office under
Fox, and the Home Office under Shelburne. By no means all these measures
were uncongenial to the King, but the new ministry lacked stability. Rockingham
and Shelburne bickered over patronage. Even worse, Shelburne and Fox
quarrelled over America. This would have mattered less had not the colonies
come under the Home Office, which meant that both men were actively
involved in the peace negotiations. Since recognition of Independence was more
or less the only card Britain had to play, Shelburne thought it should only be
conceded at the successful conclusion of negotiations. The headstrong Fox was
for recognizing it right away. At the end of June the Cabinet came down in
support of Shelburne. Fox threatened to resign. At this point on 1 July 1783
Rockingham died.

Rockingham's death must have appeared fortuitous to the King because
it made it possible to edge Fox out of the ministry. The King loathed Fox's
immorality and overt desire to lessen the power of the Crown. Shelburne became
Prime Minister and Fox went into opposition. Intriguingly, in view of future
events, George III suggested the twenty-three-year-old William Pitt, the son of
Chatham, as Home Secretary. In fact he became Chancellor of the Exchequer.
However, if Rockingham had lived, Fox's ability to create mischief might have
been kept in check. Now there was no one to restrain him. A week later, on
9 July, when Parliament rose for the summer he launched a violent attack on
the ministry and, by implication, the King. George III commented, 'The mask

is certainly cast off; it is no less than a struggle whether I am to be dictated to by Mr. Fox.'

It soon became clear that Shelburne had too little support in Parliament to proceed alone and he began to cast about unsuccessfully for support. In February 1783 he lost several votes in the Commons and on the 24th resigned. The ambition of the King, who was never really reconciled to party politics, was to try and form what amounted to a National Government, in which all were represented. To this end, he approached Pitt the Younger, then North. However, in the middle of February Fox and North had entered into private discussions and found that if they combined their forces they were powerful enough to force themselves on the King or, as it was called, 'to storm the Closet'. George does not seem fully to have understood what was happening. He was not the only person who found such a surprising union hard to grasp. The choice of Fox and North for Prime Minister was the nominal leader of the Rockingham Whigs, the Duke of Portland. This they put to George III. After another desperate appeal to Pitt, and again considering the notion of abdication, George had no option but to submit. On 2 April the new ministers, as was the tradition, kissed his hand on their formal appointment.

The King was outraged by this turn of events. He considered the new administration 'the most daring and unprincipled faction that the annals of this kingdom ever produced'. The day before he had outlined to Grenville's son, Lord Temple, what his attitude to it would be – one of armed neutrality. 'A ministry which I have avowedly attempted to avoid ... cannot be supposed to have either my favour or my confidence.' George III had parted on friendly terms from North in 1782 but had since been aggrieved to discover that North had neglected to complete the Secret Service Accounts for his last two years in office

Opposite: William Pitt the Younger,
George III's eleventh and thirteenth
Prime Minister, between 1783 and 1801,
and again from 1804 to 1806. Portrait
by John Hoppner, 1804–5.
National Portrait Gallery

and furthermore had left unpaid £30,000 he had borrowed on George's behalf. The King, himself meticulous in business, badly overreacted to these sins of omission and most unjustly accused North of malpractice. His distaste for Fox was more soundly based. Fox's father, the 1st Baron Holland, was the most despised politician of his age. He had amassed a fortune as Paymaster General and was a byword for cynical jobbery and venality. He represented all that George III had sought to expunge from public life. His second son, Charles James, though a man of much higher political principles – unfortunately, they were mostly strongly opposed to the King's – led a life of such dissipation, of reckless gambling and insouciant whoring, that it must have caused George III to shudder. He also made no effort to disguise his contempt for the King, whom in general conversation he often referred to as 'a blockhead' or 'Satan'. No wonder, if the account of Lord John Townshend, nephew of Charles Townshend, is to be believed, that when he kissed hands George III 'turned back his eyes and ears like the horse at Astley's when the tailor he had determined to throw was getting on him', though not the least revealing part of this *jeu d'esprit* is that a leading Whig could picture his sovereign as a circus animal.

However, the King was not alone in regarding the union between Fox and North as against the natural order of things. Even in the eighteenth century, with its reputation for political cynicism, this seemed a step too far. Fox had spent the last decade denouncing North's American policy. How, in good faith, could they now share the government of the country between them? The coalition of the two men was widely perceived as grotesque. Nor did Fox, in particular, display any tact in his conduct of office. He further alienated George III by taking the part of the Prince of Wales in a squabble over the Prince's finances. Fox then embarked on an ambitious attempt to reform the East India Company. This was

Opposite: 'Carlo Khan' – Charles James
Fox rides to East India House in
Leadenhall Street to seize control of the
riches of the East, a lampoon of his East
India Bill, by James Sayers, 1783.
British Museum

certainly necessary, but the plan he came up with was seen by his opponents as
an attempt to place the enormous power and patronage of the Company in the
hands of the ministry, in other words of Fox himself. This might have been unfair
but Fox was a politician and should have been alive to such concerns.

On 3 December 1783 the East India Bill was passed by the Commons.
The King, who had been biding his time, now struck. He had been carrying on
private negotiations with Pitt and knew that were he offered the post of First
Minister the young man would accept. When the Bill went up to the Lords the
King authorized Lord Temple to let it be known that 'whoever voted for the India
Bill were not only not his friends but he should consider them as his enemies'.
On 17 December the Bill was duly thrown out. There was fury in the Commons.
The next day it passed two resolutions that this reporting of the King's opinion
was 'a high crime and misdemeanour' and that any minister who supported the
dissolution of Parliament was 'an enemy to his country'. That evening the King
sent North a brief note: 'Lord North is by this required to send me the Seals of his
department, and to acquaint Mr. Fox to send those of the Foreign department ...
I choose this method as audiences on such occasions must be unpleasant.' The
following day, the 19th, Pitt kissed the King's hand as his new Prime Minister.

George III was under no illusion about the significance of what he had
done or, indeed, its possible consequences. As he remarked to Pitt, 'To one on
the edge of a precipice every ray of hope must be pleasing'. However, he was
fortified by his belief that 'each branch of the legislature has its fixed bounds ...
the executive power is vested in the Crown, and not to be infringed by
the Commons'. Equally, the King's minister had to enjoy the support of the
Commons. If this could not be obtained, then he was surely right in his
fear that 'the constitution of this country cannot subsist'.

o Khan's triumphal Entry into Leadenhall Street.

Charles James Fox addressing the
House of Commons during Pitt the
Younger's ministry, painted by Anton
Hickel, late eighteenth century.
www.bridgeman.co.uk

Pitt, at first, had a difficult ride. He had problems forming a Government
and suffered regular defeats in the Commons. On 24 March 1784 George III rode
in state to Westminster and dissolved Parliament. The ensuing election was a
triumph for the King and a disaster for Fox. Everywhere Fox's supporters were
routed. In his own constituency, Westminster, Fox barely scraped in. In part this
was a verdict on the Fox–North coalition but above all it was the nation's answer,
a resounding one, to the question: should the government of Britain be

appointed by the King or
by Fox? The response was so
decisive that Pitt, the King's
choice as minister, was to remain
in office for seventeen years.

The events of 1783–84 provide
a penetrating insight into the King's
standing in the country. He had presided
over an administration which had just
conducted a disastrous war ending in a humiliating peace. He had then opposed
and dismissed a ministry forced on him by the Commons. It might have been
expected that he would have forfeited his personal popularity and compromised
the position of the Crown. Instead, he emerged with his power and influence
greater than at any time since his accession. The country as a whole had rallied
round their monarch. Whatever the American colonists might have thought, his
British subjects judged him a Prince supremely fit to be the ruler of a free
people. The irony of the American War of Independence is that it led to the
eventual collapse not of the British monarchy but of the French.

Having found in Pitt, as he had in North, a satisfactory minister to conduct
the nation's business, George III was able to revert to his role of encouraging and
advising his Government. He must have thought, at times, that he had more
control over this than he did over his own family. His brothers, the Dukes of
Gloucester and Cumberland, had made wildly unsuitable marriages and, as a
result, in 1772 the King had forced the Royal Marriages Act through a restive
Parliament so that his consent would be needed to render any future such
marriage legal. Now, however, his own sons were growing to manhood. George,

Prince of Wales, was proving particularly difficult. He was adept at involving himself with loose women and spending large sums of money. George III was shocked by the former and embarrassed by the latter. Like all Hanoverian heirs, the Prince soon allied himself with the opposition. When, in October 1788, the ill-health the King had suffered that summer began to turn to derangement it created a serious political crisis. If there were a need for a Regent, precedent dictated it should be the Prince of Wales, but it was widely acknowledged the Prince would turn out the present Tory ministers and bring in his own Whig friends. As a consequence, in the Parliamentary debates on the subject, there was a curious reversal of roles. The Tories argued for a strictly limited Regency, while the Whigs asserted that the Prince as Regent should have untrammelled powers. Fortunately, by the end of February 1789 the King had recovered. Previously unaware of the crisis of which he had been the cause, the King was decidedly unhappy to discover the role played by his son.

From 1789 until the onset of George III's final illness at the end of 1810, events at both home and abroad were to be dominated by the outbreak and consequences of the French Revolution, which pitted the French people against its ancient monarchy. In its early stages this had seemed relatively benign. Many Britons prided themselves that the French were going to adapt a constitution modelled on the British. Alas, by 1793, they had abolished not only monarchy, but diplomacy, civility and even common humanity, and were at war with most of Europe. The execution of Louis XVI sent shock waves across the Continent. In Britain, the Whigs split into moderate and radical factions. Burke, whose 1790 essay *Reflections on the Revolution in France* – 'a good book,' the King thought, 'every gentleman ought to read it' – had been prescient, was an early defector. Pitt even negotiated with Fox about the possibility of co-operation but to no effect. However, in 1794, many of the Whigs under the Duke of Portland joined the Government. The small rump that was left felt so ineffective that in the late 1790s they actually seceded from Parliament.

George III had welcomed the outbreak of hostilities with France. He thought armed force the only means of dealing with 'that unprincipled country, whose aim at present is to destroy the foundations of every civilized state'. The war did not, however, go well. A British expedition to the Low Countries under the Duke of York was a failure and this set the pattern for the next decade. The British fleet could dominate the ocean, but on land she and her allies in Europe proved powerless to halt French aggression. There was also a threat from within Britain itself. While a huge majority of the population shared the King's horror at events in France, radical hotheads espoused her as a model for the future of the country. The one most remembered today is Tom Paine, who described George III as a man in a gold wig. Some of the ruling classes, too, flirted with the new ideas.

With hindsight, it is clear the Government's reaction was uncalled for. Indeed, the persecution and prosecution of some of the radicals may have been counterproductive. At the time, however, official nervousness was understandable. Widespread economic distress was leading to unrest. In 1795 there were bread riots, not only in Coventry and Nottingham but also in Birmingham, where a mere four years earlier a mob had destroyed the house of Joseph Priestley, the radical dissenter, in the name of 'Church and King'. It was, of course, bread riots which had set off the French Revolution. Now, Pitt's house was attacked and when George III drove to the State Opening of Parliament in October he had to brave a howling mob shouting 'No King! Down with George!' Parson Woodforde witnessed the occasion: 'saw the King go in his State Coach drawn with eight fine Cream-Coloured Horses in red Morocco-leather Harness, to the House of Lords ... his Majesty was very grossly insulted by some of the Mob, and had a very narrow escape of being killed going to the House, a Ball passing thro' the Windows as he went thro' old Palace-Yard, supposed to be discharged from an air Gun, but very fortunately did not strike the King or Lords. On his return from the House to [St.] James's Palace he was very much hissed & hooted at, and on his going from St. James's to the Queen's Palace in his private Coach, he had another very lucky escape, as the Mob surrounded his Coach and one of them was going to open the Door but the Horse Guards coming up very providentially at the Time prevented any further disorder. The State-Coach Windows going from St. James's to the Mews were broke all to pieces by the Mob ... The Mob was composed of the most violent & lowest Democrats. Thank God the King received no injury whatever ... Every Person attached to his Majesty was very much alarmed and concerned for him to-day. It was said that there were near two hundred thousand People in St. James Park, about 3 o'clock. I never was in such a croud in all my Life.' Despite this uproar George III was remarkably composed and read his Speech from the Throne as if nothing had happened. The riot also called forth evidence of strong support for the King. The next evening when he and Queen Charlotte went to Covent Garden Theatre he was enthusiastically received and 'God Save the King' was played six times.

The year before, in 1794, Pitt had already begun to introduce a series of repressive measures to counter the perceived threat from revolutionaries, including the suspension of Habeas Corpus, an ancient common-law right enshrined in statute law in 1679, which prevented arbitrary detention and imprisonment. This move was fiercely opposed by the Whigs. When in 1797 the fleet mutinied at Spithead, off Portsmouth, and the Nore, off Sheerness in the Thames Estuary, the Government's worst fears of a general popular rising seemed to be coming true. Such were official sensitivities that in 1798 the King was to have Fox's name struck from the Privy Council for toasting 'Our sovereign, the people'. While troubling, all these events proved to be distractions. The real problem, as so often in British history, was Ireland.

Ireland had been feared in the seventeenth century as a limitless source of Catholic troops which the Stuart kings might use to buttress their prerogative. In fact, the failure of the Stuart cause, both in the Civil War and at the Glorious Revolution, was disastrous for the Irish. Ireland ended the century with her Catholic population stripped of its political rights and much of its land. Most power and wealth were concentrated in the hands of a relatively small number of Protestants, known as The Ascendancy. There was also a group of poorer Protestants, mainly from Scotland, who had settled chiefly in Ulster. Though the Irish Parliament had been granted considerable legislative autonomy in 1782, many Catholics and some Ulster Protestants were disaffected. What was more, with the outbreak of the Revolutionary Wars in Europe Britain again needed Irish troops. The French were well aware that Ireland was Britain's Achilles heel and in 1798 planned an invasion. This was meant to coincide with a rising in Ireland. In the event both the invasion and the rising were miserable failures but the British Government was nevertheless rattled. Pitt came round to the view that the only solution to governing Ireland was its legislative union with Britain. This duly took place in 1801 with the creation of the United Kingdom of Great Britain and Ireland. In the long term the results of the Union were singularly unhappy. It bedevilled Anglo-Irish relations throughout the nineteenth and twentieth centuries. In the short term its creation led to the fall of the Government.

Pitt had wanted to couple the Union with Catholic emancipation. This restoration of their political rights would have allowed eligible Catholics to vote and to sit in Parliament. George III was appalled. He was not himself particularly anti-Catholic, but he was the representative of a dynasty that had been called to the throne to ensure that Catholics played no part in the political life of the nation. In addition, at his Coronation, he had sworn a solemn oath to this effect, assenting that he would 'to the utmost of ... [his] power maintain the laws of God ... and the Protestant Reformed Religion established by Law'. He did not see how he could set this oath aside. This was not affectation or pretence. The vows he had taken were often in his mind and he frequently referred to them. Twenty years earlier, when after the American War he considered abdicating, the draft speech to Parliament he prepared contained the sentence which sums up his own estimate of his rule and the constraints upon it: 'My obedience to the oath I took at my coronation prevents my exceeding the powers vested in me, or submitting to be a cipher in the trammels of any self-created band.' In 1795 when the then Lord Lieutenant of Ireland, Lord Fitzwilliam, appeared to promise Irish Catholics a degree of emancipation, George had been troubled enough to consult Lord Kenyon, the Lord Chief Justice, about his oath.

Indeed, it is Pitt whose conduct here is difficult to understand. Knowing the King as he did, he could scarcely have imagined that he would ever agree to the measure. At the end of January 1801 the King let it be known that he would regard anyone who voted for emancipation as his enemy. In this he was in accord with his subjects outside Ireland. As the politician and wit Lord Dudley remarked ruefully as the end of the decade, 'upon that subject it [the country] is just as obstinate as his Majesty', and Lord John Russell, one of the next generation of Whigs and a future Prime Minister, was to lament, 'unfortunately ... the prejudices which the Sovereign cherished in his own bosom, were widely diffused throughout the nation ... he was followed with such sympathy by his people that for nearly twenty years after he ceased to rule ... [Catholic emancipation] still remained unaccomplished.' Pitt accordingly resigned. The King commissioned the Speaker of the House of Commons, Henry Addington, to form a ministry. George III then fell ill. Addington was not able to kiss hands on taking office until 17 March. To aid the King's recovery Pitt seems to have promised him that he would never again raise the dreaded subject.

Addington was widely known as 'The Doctor', an unkind reference to his father's profession, and Canning was to sum up his lack of stature compared with his predecessor in the quip: 'Pitt is to Addington /As London is to Paddington'. However, George III was fond of him and Pitt, who after seventeen years seems almost to have been relieved to be out of office, promised to support him. Then in 1802, there was a lull in the hostilities with France. The Peace of Amiens was signed on 27 March. George III had little hope for this and regarded it as an experimental peace, which is what it proved to be.

Continued French expansion in Europe and general lack of trust of Napoleon Bonaparte's intentions led to war being declared again in May 1803. For a year there was a major invasion scare. Though old and increasingly infirm, the King was determined to be at the head of his troops. On 26 and 28 October he reviewed 27,000 volunteers in Hyde Park. On each day, half a million members of the public were estimated to have been present. The King had made preparations that if the French army landed in Kent he would go to Dartford, if in Essex to Chelmsford. Should the enemy succeed in approaching too close to Windsor, he determined to send the Queen and the Princesses to his old friend Bishop Hurd at Worcester. In the event, the French force did not attempt to cross

The GRAND R.

The Prince and his party were drove to the Summit of a hill where they made a stand for pear
favoured their flight is left the several battalions masters of the field his Majesty followed

SYDENHAM COMMON

but where at length Obliged to retreat to the bottom setting fire to the furze & hedges the Smoke of which
at the head of a troop of dragoons to the foot of the hill when he remounted & returned back to the Lines.

Previous page: 'The Grand Review on Sydenham Common', by Isaac Cruikshank, 1792. King George was determined to head his troops and often reviewed them in person, though here his enemies are the Prince of Wales and Charles James Fox.
Guildhall Library, Corporation of London

the Channel and Nelson's annihilation of the French fleet at Trafalgar in 1805 ensured that they never would.

In the meantime, the Prince of Wales succeeded in causing George III as much embarrassment as Napoleon. Just as George III had in his youth, the Prince demanded that he be allowed to serve in the army, especially at this time of national emergency. And, as George II refused this request so did George III. In vexation and one of his many displays of irresponsible self-indulgence, the Prince of Wales published his letters and the King's replies in the London papers. George III was outraged. In 1804 he had another attack of illness. Thomas Creevey, the Whig M.P., wrote him off: 'The fact is I believe … that the Regal function will never more be exercised by him.' There was an element of wishful thinking in this, driven by political ambition. 'God send we may have a Regency', Creevey prayed. Heartless as this was, it expressed the feeling the Whigs had harboured for over twenty years. They saw the incapacity of George III as their only hope of securing power. In fact, the King recovered just in time to confront a fresh political squall, which he handled with some firmness.

Though he still enjoyed the confidence of the King, Addington was not skilful enough to maintain the support of the Commons. Pitt, who had come to resent his successor, had turned against him and in a most unexpected development had allied himself with Fox. The Doctor's ministry duly foundered. George III had no problem with Pitt's return to office, especially as in April 1804 Pitt had assured him, once again, that he would propose no measures that would be objectionable to the King. George III was even prepared to accept the Foxites. He did, however, draw the line at Fox himself. Consequently, when Pitt took office on 10 May he did not enjoy the support of either Fox or his followers and he was to be hard pressed in the Commons. Nor did the war against the newly

proclaimed French Emperor, or 'usurper' as the King regarded him, go well. True, at sea the French and Spanish fleets were destroyed by Nelson at Trafalgar on 21 October 1805, but the coalition of Austria and Russia which Pitt had encouraged and financed was decisively defeated by Napoleon at Austerlitz on 2 December. Pitt was in no state to withstand such a blow. Though only forty-six, his health was failing and on 23 January 1806 he died.

On 11 February Lord Grenville kissed hands as Prime Minister. He was the third and most talented of the sons of George Grenville. The most significant member of the ministry was the Secretary of State for Foreign Affairs, none other than Charles James Fox. After some initial resistance the King proved remarkably relaxed about his appointment. When he received him, George III observed: 'Mr. Fox, I little thought you and I should ever meet again in this place,' but assured him he had no wish to dwell on old grievances. Despite Fox's desire to negotiate peace with France, the King got on remarkably well with his *bête noir*. Neither man was in good health. Perhaps both were weary of their long battles. It would be pleasing to record that they were able to make a new beginning.

It was not to be. In June, Fox fell ill and nothing the doctors were able to do could save him. On 13 September he died. Fox's devoted nephew and political heir, Lord Holland, asserted that the King 'could hardly suppress his indecent exultation at his death'. He was quite wrong. Perhaps even George III was surprised by his own reaction. He remarked to Addington, 'Little did I think I should ever live to regret Mr Fox's death.'

Grenville's ministry was reconstructed after this catastrophe but did not survive long in its new form. In 1793 Pitt had legislated to allow Roman Catholics in Ireland to hold military commissions up to the rank of Colonel. Grenville now proposed that this concession be extended to Great Britain. What the King discovered, however, was that the legislation would also allow Catholics to hold commissions above the rank of Colonel. There was some dispute about whether he had been informed of this. In any event, he not only refused to countenance it but also insisted on a promise from his ministers not to raise the Catholic issue again. They refused and went out of office. The King turned instead to the Duke of Portland, who had briefly been Prime Minister in 1783. Then he had presided over the Fox–North coalition which had given so much offence to the King. With the passing of the years, however, the Duke had, though still a Whig, become more conservative and by the time he kissed hands to return to the position of Prime Minister on 31 March 1807, George III regarded him as an old and valued friend. He served for two and a half years, resigning shortly before his death on 30 October 1809. The King replaced him with the Chancellor of the Exchequer, Spencer Perceval, having first assured himself that Perceval had no intention of raising the Catholic question. Though neither the King nor the country knew it, this was the last time he was to choose a First Minister.

George III viewing Napoleon as a
Lilliputian – a slight on Napoleon's
stature and a reflection of the British
public's view of him; a cartoon by
James Gillray.
The British Library, 754.a.6, opp. p.13

5

All monarchs are mirrors which their
subjects hold up to see themselves ...

The image and achievement of the King 1760–1820

A King is not just a political animal, a reign not just a collection of historical occurrences that happen to occupy the dates between accession and death. All monarchs are mirrors which their subjects hold up to see themselves, and those sovereigns who best reflect the virtues which their people hold in highest esteem often have the greatest influence. This is particularly true of George III. He was not a natural politician. His character was too straightforward for that, the uncharitable might have said 'too simple'. He heartily disliked the arts of politics and regarded most of the jockeying for power as mere 'faction'. Indeed, for the first ten years of his reign, there was much to be said for this view. George had a fixed set of beliefs which changed very little throughout his life. His contemporaries and subsequent historians judged his reign a failure or a success depending on whether or not they shared these beliefs. However, though only two centuries have passed, the political circumstances of his era are now so remote that it is the other aspects of the King's life and character that command attention. It is these more personal characteristics which explain why George III had so powerful a hold on the affections of so many of his subjects.

Underlying everything George did was a profound and sincere Christian belief. The later eighteenth century is often seen as an age of scepticism and cynicism. In some circles it was. Intellectual doubts had gained hold. Some of the century's greatest thinkers and writers, for instance David Hume and Edward Gibbon, were avowed atheists. Many amongst the upper classes treated religion as little more than a social necessity. You sent your servants to church in order that they should not murder you. It did not affect your own conduct. Meanwhile, the established church was portrayed as complacent and corrupt. But these were mere ripples on the surface of an ocean of faith and on all sides there were signs of religious revival. George III was a stickler for religious observance. This was not

Previous page: George III and
Queen Charlotte preside over the
distribution of the Maundy Money,
S.H. Grimm, 1773. George gave

Page 81: The 'Copper Horseman' at
Windsor, commissioned by George's
son, George IV, and sculpted by
Sir Richard Westmacott.
Guildhall Library, Corporation of London

much of his income to charities and
beneficiaries, demonstrating a very
practical and generous care for his
subjects.
The British Library, K. Top. XXVI.5

a matter of social conformity. It was because, like the majority of his subjects, he believed quite literally what was written in the Bible and he saw it as his duty to follow its precepts. This was the reason he characterized the atheist Voltaire as 'a monster'.

As has been seen, almost his very first act as King was to issue a proclamation against vice. Unlike his predecessors or his immediate successors, George III led a life of blameless domestic virtue and he tried to ensure that others followed suit. The victorious Nelson was snubbed at court after his triumph at the Battle of the Nile because of the King's disapproval of his scandalous relationship with Lady Hamilton. George III also did his best to see that clerical offices were held with propriety and bestowed only on those he deemed fit. At the behest of the Methodist Countess of Huntingdon he reproved an Archbishop of Canterbury, Frederick Cornwallis, for his lavish hospitality at Lambeth Palace. He actually frustrated Pitt the Younger's desire that his tutor, Bishop Tomline, should be elevated to the see of Canterbury because he thought the Dean of Windsor, Charles Manners-Sutton, a better man. Though strongly committed to the Church of England's health and well-being, he was, however, prepared to override it on occasion. As the poet Coleridge observed of 'our late good old King', George III thought every adult in the British Empire should be able to read the Bible and have a Bible to read. Because of this the King was prepared to endorse the educational work of the Quaker Joseph Lancaster, the advocate of the Monitorial System in which the elder pupils taught the younger, much to the annoyance of many Anglicans.

The King's religion was of the practical sort. He devoted a good part of his income to charities and benefactions of all kinds. This extended far beyond institutionalized acts of royal largesse, such as giving alms to poor pensioners on

Maundy Thursday. When, during his first illness at the end of the 1780s, a committee was appointed to examine the Privy Purse, it was discovered that out of a then private income of £80,000 a year George III gave away £14,000 to charity. In 1809, to mark the beginning of his fiftieth year on the throne, he presented £6,000 to be distributed for the relief of the poor prisoners and debtors in his three kingdoms. He was a firm admirer of John Howard, the penal reformer, giving money to improve prison buildings. So impressed was he by the man that after meeting him, he declared, 'Howard wants no statue. His virtues will live when every statue has crumbled into dust.' Despite this, he later headed a subscription for a statue to him though this was never erected because, as it happened, Howard agreed with the King.

In other ways, George III practised what he preached. He himself considered he had been indolent as a child. This seems unlikely but, if he were, he certainly made up for it in adult life. He was assiduous in his attention to business and his reputation for industry led to many stories. For example, Sir Walter Scott was told by Lord Bathurst, one of his ministers, that the King made it a matter of principle to read every word of every Act of Parliament submitted to him. Even if this may be doubted, his workload was undoubtedly large and since, until almost the end of his active life, he had no secretary, he conducted all his correspondence himself. His quest for precision can be seen in the way most of his letters carry the exact time: 'Queen's House, 38 min. past 7 o'clock', 'Windsor, 26 min. past 8 p.m.'. Not the least of his torments on falling ill was that he was unable to pay proper attention to the official despatches. In an age when many men were slaves to their senses, the King was addicted to duty.

His tastes were simple, even austere. In his later years his private rooms had bare board floors, since he thought carpets dust traps. His preference was for

King George's writing desk, where
he spent many hours occupied with
matters of state. Until 1805 he had no
secretary and dealt with the great mass
of official papers himself.
Museum of London

plain, even very plain, food. When the King visited Lord Coventry at Croome
Court in Worcestershire, now renowned as the site of Capability Brown's first
landscape garden, a contemporary noted that he dined on salmon, which he said
was the best he had ever tasted, potted lamprey – an eel-like fish, presumably
from the River Severn nearby – and venison. Carp was also served and the King
drank two glasses of port. But here George III was a guest and he was being
entertained in style. Normally for dinner he would eat only a meat course with
a little fruit after. He was also said to like sauerkraut. With such a repast he drank
a sort of lemonade he called 'cup'. One of his equerries, Colonel Goldsworthy,

'Temperance Enjoying a Frugal Meal',
by James Gillray, 1792. The cartoon
conveys George and Charlotte's
preference for plain food.
National Portrait Gallery

famously expressed his mortification at spending a hard day in the saddle attending the King only to be offered barley-water by George III to revive him. Like George VI, who insisted that the Royal Family observe the same food rationing as the nation in the Second World War, George III was equally prepared to lead the way in a crisis. When poor harvests in the mid 1790s led to unrest, Queen Charlotte informed the Prince of Wales 'The Kg. also has given orders ... to have no other bread served to the Household & even to his own table *than brown bread*, & it is to be hoped that this will encourage others to do the same.' The Queen boasted that the King had even experimented with potato bread 'which proves to be remarcably good'.

This austerity extended to his life as a whole. Pierre Jean Grosley, a French visitor to England in the first decade of his reign, remarked that most of George III's nobility lived on a grander scale than their monarch. On his accession the King had agreed to a Civil List of £800,000 a year, over £70,000 less than his grandfather had enjoyed in the last year of his reign. Out of this all the expenses of the civil administration had to be paid. From it, the King on his accession allocated to himself a private income of £48,000 a year, though this sum rose during his reign. These figures were not high. The fifth Duke of Devonshire, who succeeded to his title in 1764, was reckoned to have an income of £35,000 a year. In consequence both the King and the Queen fell into debt. Successive applications had to be made to Parliament. One M.P. in the late 1760s, ignoring the chronic underfunding of the Crown's public and private expenses, gave voice to a widespread but totally unfounded suspicion that the money must be going to buy influence in Parliament. In fact, George III managed his own money with meticulous care and, though some of the Civil List may have seeped away through supporting outdated offices which had long become sinecures, the

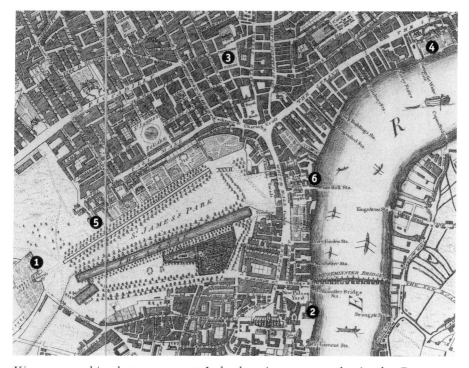

King was anything but extravagant. Indeed, society came to despise the Court as dowdy and the King's subjects laughed at his frugality. Many prints and printed satires, such as those of 'Peter Pindar', the pseudonym of the physician John Wolcot, poked gentle fun at George. Queen Charlotte was thought to be particularly stingy and, although the middle classes laughed, they also approved. The expensive excesses of the aristocracy masked the growing seriousness of a large body of the population. Although it was not his motivation George III was very much in tune with the times.

Opposite: Windsor Castle, George's favourite residence, where he commissioned much restoration and new building during his reign. From W.H. Pyne, *The History of the Royal Residences* (1819). *The British Library. 60.g.11, opp. p.83*

Below: The Queen's House, rebuilt by George III's successors as Buckingham Palace. From W.H. Pyne, *The History of the Royal Residences* (1819). *The British Library, 747.f.3, opp. p.1*

On what, then, did the King spend his money? George III, as it has turned out, established which were to be the leading royal residences in the future. In London the Court was based at St James's, originally built by Henry VIII and, after the burning down of most of Whitehall Palace in 1698, the official home of the monarch. George III was married there, as was his son, George IV, who had been born there. However, from William III onwards, sovereigns had tended to divide their time between Kensington Palace and Hampton Court. Perhaps because both of these had unhappy associations with his grandfather, George II, George III never used them. In the capital in 1762 he bought Buckingham House at the west end of St James's Park for £28,000 from the illegitimate son of John Sheffield, Duke of Buckingham. He and the Queen moved into it in September 1763. It was known as 'The Queen's House', although only transferred to Queen Charlotte for the duration of her life in 1775 in exchange for Somerset House, which had been the official residence of the Queen Consort since the accession of James I and VI in 1603.

The King occupied the ground floor of the Queen's House, while the Queen had the rooms above on the first floor. The house itself was reasonably modest. As George III's family and collections grew, it had to be extended. The

garden front originally had eleven windows. The library extension to the south
and the new domestic rooms to the north, which were constructed between 1766
and 1768, each added a further seven to this tally. For the first time the sovereign
became, in Creevey's words, 'the Gentleman at the end of the Mall'. However,
the King would not recognize Buckingham Palace as it stands today. It was totally
reconstructed by John Nash for George IV. Major works continued for over
thirty years and, after George III, the first sovereign to live there was Queen
Victoria. The famous east front facing the Mall dates only from 1913.

    The King, however, did not care for life in London, preferring instead a
home within easy reach of the capital. His father had settled at Kew, a village on
the River Thames seven miles to the west of London. Here it was that Alexander
Pope presented Frederick with a dog whose collar bore the famous epigram 'I am
his Highness' dog at Kew; / Pray, tell me sir, whose dog are you?' George and his

mother had continued to live there after Prince Frederick's death. The Princess occupied the White House, somewhat grandiloquently known as Kew Palace, while her son lived at Richmond Lodge nearby. On the Princess's death, George III and Queen Charlotte themselves moved into the White House. It was far too small for their growing family, and their sons had to live in the adjoining Dutch House, the present Kew Palace. In 1802 the King had the White House demolished and commissioned a Castellated Palace to the 'Gothic' designs of the architect James Wyatt. This ill-starred and, by all accounts, highly impractical building was never completed due to the King's illness and was subsequently demolished.

Kew was Queen Charlotte's favourite home. Indeed, she was to die at the Dutch House. Whether it would have continued the seat of royalty if the Castellated Palace had been completed cannot be known, but the King had already transferred his affections to a new location. Windsor Castle, twenty-five miles west of London, was the most ancient of the royal residences. Steeped in history, the Castle had been started under William the Conqueror. From it, King John had ridden out to meet the Barons at Runnymede and assent to Magna Carta. Edward III had made it the focus of his cult of knighthood. It had been extensively altered by Charles II, but after the death of Queen Anne had fallen into neglect. In the mid 1770s, Queen Charlotte asked to be given the Queen's Lodge adjoining the Castle, where Queen Anne had lived. It was a decision she was to regret because it encouraged and confirmed her husband's increasing enthusiasm for Windsor. He began major works repairing the fifteenth-century St George's Chapel. By 1786 the restoration of the State Apartments was completed. Finally, the King commissioned James Wyatt to provide new private apartments for the Royal Family within the Castle itself. These were ready by the end of 1804.

From the 1780s the Royal Family spent more time at Windsor than Kew. The King founded farms in the Great Park, which flourish today. He bought property in the town and ensured that a theatre was established there. He supported the famous school across the river at Eton, founded by his Lancastrian predecessor Henry VI. Its pupils still celebrate George III's birthday, 4 June, as a holiday. Like any great landowner, he took a personal interest in the borough's parliamentary elections. He and his family became familiar figures in the town and its vicinity. The King walked about largely unattended and made a point of talking to everyone he met. He was in his element as the benevolent local squire. Many of George III's works on the Castle were destroyed or overlaid by George IV, who with his architect Wyatville transformed the Castle into the Gothic fort that exists today. However, the increasing role which Windsor was to occupy in royal life was demonstrated by George III's decision that he and his family would be buried there rather than, as was traditional, at Westminster Abbey. Between 1804 and 1810 a new royal vault was constructed under the Tomb House of St George's Chapel. The first person to be interred there, in 1810, was George's daughter Amelia and the bodies of his young sons Octavius and Alfred were removed there from Westminster. It was fitting, therefore, that after his own death George IV should celebrate his father's attachment to the place by commissioning, in 1824, a great equestrian statue of the King, the famous 'Copper Horseman', from Sir Richard Westmacott. Erected in 1831 on Snow Hill at the end of the long walk, George III, arrayed somewhat incongruously as the 'good' Emperor Marcus Aurelius, has gazed out ever since over the domain he loved.

As well as being an enthusiastic if not, despite the lessons he had received from Sir William Chambers, an entirely successful devotee of architecture, the King was also an eager collector and patron of the arts. Even in his own lifetime,

Opposite: Extract from a letter from
George, published under his pseudonym
Ralph Robinson, in *The Annals of
Agriculture*. His homes at Kew and
Windsor had profitable working farms
in which he took great interest.
The British Library, 255.a.7, p.65

this aspect of his reign went relatively unremarked. Abroad it was the era of the
benevolent despots – enlightened royal reformers who, like the King's cousin
Frederick the Great of Prussia or the remarkable Catherine the Great of Russia,
corresponded with and entertained the leading *philosophes* of the day. George III,
by contrast, has always enjoyed a reputation for dullness. The 1832 edition of
The Extraordinary Black Book, the compilation of the radical journalist John Wade,
which advertised itself as exposing abuses in church and state, declared
condescendingly, 'the mental endowments of the king were very moderate, and
he possessed no strength or originality of mind'. It is true George III had a very
English dislike of abstract thought. 'None of your Scotch metaphysics,' he
commanded Henry Dundas, the Secretary of State for War, in a turn of phrase
that would have delighted Dr Johnson, who disdained both Scotsmen and
metaphysics. He also famously told the novelist Fanny Burney that much of
Shakespeare was 'stuff ... Only one must not say so! ... what? ... what?' In fact,
George was a voracious reader, with an excellent knowledge of literature. But
the King did not claim to be an original thinker. He was in essence a well-read
country squire and his favourite pursuits were rural ones.

   Not only did he hunt – stags in preference to foxes – almost daily when in
the country, as his nick-name 'Farmer George' attests, he also cultivated the soil.
This was not the romantic escapism of a Marie Antoinette, pretending to be a
shepherdess in the make-believe setting of The Queen's Hamlet, designed for her
by the architect Mique in 1783 in the grounds of the Petit Trianon at Versailles.
At both Kew, where George III even turned some of the park over to arable
crops, and Windsor he ran working farms on which he made a profit. Under the
pseudonym of Ralph Robinson he wrote to Arthur Young's *Annals of Agriculture*,
regretting that Mr Ducket, 'the able cultivator of Petersham', had not favoured

ON MR. DUCKET's MODE OF CULTI-VATION.

By Mr. Ralph Robinson, of Windsor.

January 1, 1787.

SIR,

IT is reasonable to expect that your laudable efforts for the improvement of husbandry, by publishing the Annals of Agriculture, must in time be crowned with success ; therefore it seems incumbent on all who think they have materials on this interesting subject worthy of the inspection of the public, to transmit them to you, who, if you view them in that light, will give them a place in that estimable work.

Without further preface, I shall mention that the dispute which has lately arisen on the subject of summer fallows, had made me secretly wish that Mr. Ducket, the able cultivator of Petersham, in Surrey, would have communicated his thoughts, not only on that subject, but would have benefited the public, by a full explanation of that course of husbandry which has rendered his farm at Peter-sham, which has now been above nineteen years in his hands so flourishing, though his three prede-cessors had failed on it.

When he first entered on it, all the land, ex-cept the meadows, appeared to be hungry sand,

King George III and Queen Charlotte at
the Royal Academy of Art, surrounded
by portraits of the Royal Family.
Guildhall Library/Corporation of London

the nation with a description of how he rotated
fallow crops, clover, turnips and rye, with his
wheat, barley and oats. George was also one
of the pioneers who introduced Merino sheep
from Spain into England. Napoleon's dictum
was wrong. England was less a nation of
shopkeepers than one of farmers. Farming
was still the dominant occupation amongst
all classes of the nation and the King's subjects
were flattered that in pursuing this interest
he was truly 'one of them'.

George III's rural enthusiasms have helped
to disguise the fact that he was much better
educated than most of his aristocrats and had a
lively and inquiring mind. As a monarch it may
have been his duty but it was also clearly his
pleasure to invest large amounts of both his time
and money in promoting the cultural well-
being of his kingdoms. In 1768, he underwrote
the foundation of the Royal Academy of Arts to
the extent of £5,000, declaring that he would
be its 'patron, protector and supporter'. Though
he disliked the artist Sir Joshua Reynolds, its
first President, he ensured that the Academy was
given rooms in both the old Somerset House
and Sir William Chambers's new building which

replaced it on The Strand. He made a point of attending its exhibitions. In 1762 he had purchased for £20,000 the collections of Joseph Smith, British Consul in Venice until 1760. These included the greatest assemblage of canvases by Canaletto in the world. George III was not, however, a real connoisseur of paintings. He liked portraits because they showed his family. The enduring early image of him is the Coronation portrait, with its pair of the Queen, by Allan Ramsay, who was elevated to official portrait painter in 1767. For the rest he enjoyed paintings that told a story, especially if it were a morally improving one, and his favourite artist was the American Benjamin West.

The King also took a decided interest in the natural sciences. As a boy his tutor had been the astronomer Stephen Demainbray, and in 1768 George III appointed him Director of the new Royal Observatory at Kew. Far more important, though, was his support for the Hanoverian William Herschel. In 1781 Herschel had astonished contemporaries by discovering a planet unknown to the ancients, thereby enlarging the solar system. He called this new body *Georgium Sidus*, the Georgian Star, in honour of the King, though international scientific opinion and history have opted for the name Uranus instead. George III gave Herschel a pension of £200 a year and Herschel's sister and assistant, Caroline, a further £50. He also paid £4,000 for the astronomer to build a giant forty-foot telescope at Slough, two miles north of Windsor. With this Herschel discovered the existence of galaxies. The King was a frequent visitor. On one occasion he brought the Archbishop of Canterbury to observe its wonders, remarking, 'Come, my Lord Bishop, I will show you the way to heaven'.

This was by far the largest of what might be called the King's collection of scientific instruments. The others, now mostly preserved at the Science Museum in London, included clocks and watches, in which he had a consuming interest.

Indeed, George III actively followed the attempts of John Harrison and his son William to develop a clock accurate enough at sea to allow sailors to establish longitude. He allowed their timepiece H-5 to be tested at his Kew Observatory in 1772, and after the successful trial he set in train steps to see that Parliament pay Harrison the balance of the money denied him by the Board of Longitude on a technicality. George III was also on close terms with Sir Joseph Banks, who accompanied Captain Cook to the South Seas on the *Endeavour* and was

President of the Royal Society from 1778 to 1820. From the late 1770s the King gave Banks unofficial superintendence of his gardens at Kew. Both men were interested in the commercial exploitation of exotic plants and very soon new specimens were being sent there from all over the world. This laid the scientific foundations of the Royal Botanic Gardens as they exist today.

George III's greatest passion was music, an art to which even his philistine grandfather had been addicted. The eighteenth century was an age of musical princes. His father had played and composed, as did his cousin, Frederick the Great. George III played the harpsichord, which was to be one of his few consolations in his later clouded years, as well as the organ and the flute. In this he was sometimes accompanied at the keyboard by Bach's son, Johann Christian, the 'English Bach', who was Queen Charlotte's music master. The second half of the eighteenth century was an era of dazzling musical achievement and the King had the opportunity to hear some of its greatest musicians. In 1764 the young Mozart performed for him on both the harpsichord and organ at the Queen's House. In the 1790s Haydn twice visited London and, before his final return to Vienna in 1795, George III tried unsuccessfully to persuade him to stay by offering him summer quarters at Windsor.

However, the King's taste in music was essentially conservative. He was on the Committee and a regular attender of the 'Concerts of Antient Music'. These were held in London each winter from 1776 and a prominent place in their programmes was occupied by the works of George Frederick Handel. George II had been the patron of Handel, whom George III had met as a boy. The great composer died the year before his accession but the King remained devoted to his memory. Indeed, he much exasperated the musicologist Dr Charles Burney by insisting that the praise accorded the Master in his *General History of Music* be increased. However, one of Dr Burney's rewards was a position in the Queen's household for his daughter, the novelist, Fanny. In 1784 the King attended the centenary celebrations in Westminster Abbey of Handel's birth. He had a bust of Handel by Roubiliac in the Queen's House and amongst his proudest possessions were a harpsichord that had belonged to Handel and many of his autograph scores, including that of *The Messiah*. These had come from John Christopher Smith, who had been Handel's amanuensis, as well as a member of the household of George's mother. The scores formed part of the Royal Music Library. This was deposited in the British Museum by King George V in 1911 and was presented to it by Queen Elizabeth II in 1957. It is now amongst the treasures of The British Library.

The King's most important collection has proved to be what is still known as the King's Library. This was not his private library. He must have had books of all sorts in his various palaces, and Queen Charlotte had her own substantial collection which was sold in 1819 after her death. The aim of the King's Library was education, not entertainment. It does not, for example, possess any of the newspapers which George III read so avidly. Nor does it contain much lighter literature or fiction. It was, in embryo, a new national library. In some ways this was curious because such an institution had just been founded in Britain. The British Museum had been established in 1753 and was still essentially a collection of manuscripts and printed books, with a few natural curiosities and antiquities appended. Indeed, its Director was known as the Principal Librarian until 1898. In 1757 George II had presented this fledgling institution with the old Royal Library, a dazzling assembly of manuscripts and printed books amassed by British monarchs since the reign of Edward IV. At first, before George III began work assembling his own library, he carried on this tradition. In 1762 he purchased and presented to the Museum the Thomason Tracts, a collection of nearly 22,000 Civil War and Commonwealth tracts and news sheets assembled by George Thomason, a seventeenth-century publisher and bookseller. For many years these were known as the King's Pamphlets. There was also some exchange of personnel. In 1771 James Matthews joined the Museum from the King's Library to work on the catalogue of printed books.

By then, the King's Library, which was kept at Buckingham House, was rivalling the Museum's printed holdings. The same year that he presented the Thomason Tracts to the Museum, George III acquired for himself the library of Consul Smith. He already had as Librarian Richard Dalton, but the most important figure to work for him was Frederick Augusta Barnard, one of a family of court servants and later said, quite incorrectly, to be the King's illegitimate brother. Barnard did not take over as Librarian until 1774 but was employed much earlier. It was he who in 1767 lighted the King's way through the Queen's House with a candle to meet Dr Johnson, who occasionally used the library. This meeting, which revealed the breadth of the King's reading – they discussed amongst other things the dispute between Bishops Lowth and Warburton, which both thought little more than scholars calling one another rude names – deeply impressed Johnson. He judged the King, 'the finest gentleman I have ever seen'. When, the next year, Barnard was sent abroad on a major book-buying expedition, it led to Johnson writing him a letter of advice, clearly intended for the King's eyes. 'Of ... books, which have been often published, and diversified by various modes of impression, a royal library should have at least the most curious edition, the most splendid, and the most useful. The most curious edition is commonly the first, and the most useful may be expected among the last ... The most splendid the eye will discern.'

George III's expenditure on books was between one and two thousand
pounds a year and this sum increased with the years. Towards the end of the
King's life the cost of books and salaries was running at around £4,500 per
annum. The building works at Buckingham House to accommodate his
collection illustrate both its growth and the scale of George III's ambition.
The Great or West Library was entered from the King's bedroom. Constructed
between 1762 and 1764, it was two storeys high, sixty feet long and thirty feet

Below: Presented to the nation by George IV, the King's Library is now displayed in a six-storey glass tower which is the centrepiece of The British Library.
The British Library

Opposite: A fine rococo binding by John Baumgarten, *c.* 1774, from George III's Library.
The British Library, 30.b.17

wide. Between 1766 and 1767 the South Library and the famous Octagon Room were added to the end of it. Finally, from 1772 to 1773 the East Library was built in the angle between the Great and South Libraries. In the room above the South Library the King's collections of drawings and medals were kept, and in 1774 a second storey was added to the East Library to form a 'Marine Gallery' for the models of ships. When completed, this suite of rooms comprised just under a third of the whole house.

It is no wonder, therefore, that by the nineteenth century, the Library had achieved a momentum of its own. When the King fell ill at the end of 1810, expenditure on it was continued by his trustees and its catalogue, which was published in the 1820s, was paid for out of his estate. In 1823, George IV presented the Library to the nation, though he retained a number of prize items, including 25 incunables (books printed before 1501) given to his father by the classical scholar Jacob Bryant. The collection was allocated to the British Museum. With 65,000 volumes and 20,000 pamphlets, overnight it doubled the size of the Museum Library. Moved to Kensington Palace in 1825 during the building works transforming Buckingham House into Buckingham Palace, in 1828 it was installed in the new gallery constructed by Sir Robert Smirke to one side of old Montagu House, which was to form the east wing of the new British Museum quadrangle. This is the oldest part of the present Greek revival building on the

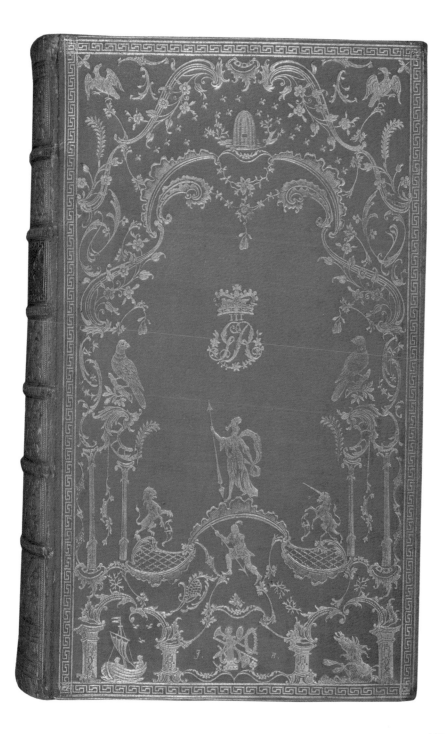

site. It met two of the requirements of the gift, that the Library should always be kept separate and should be on public display. In 1973 the British Museum Library became one of the constituent parts of the new British Library and in 1997 the King's Library was moved again, to Sir Colin St John Wilson's just completed British Library building at St Pancras. Here George III's books form the heart of the structure and, shelved in a six-storey glass book tower rising the whole height of the edifice at the rear of the Front Hall, are seen daily by all readers and visitors.

George III collected not only books but also maps and plans. Many of these were government documents and some dated back to the reign of Charles II. In addition, in 1765 the King acquired the military plans of his uncle William, Duke of Cumberland. Many of his envoys abroad sent him maps and the Board of Ordnance contributed plans of fortifications and other military buildings. The King's topographical drawings included depictions of Roman antiquities by antiquaries such as William Stukeley, as well as watercolours of the Lake District and of Welsh, Scottish and Irish mountain scenery. The official origin of many of these items and the fact that some were still sensitive led to problems when, in due course, the King's Library was presented to the nation. In the event only the King's Topographical Collection went directly to the British Museum. The Military Collection is still retained by the Crown at Windsor and the Maritime Collection was sent to the Admiralty, though much of this came to the Museum in 1844. Furthermore, the Ordnance insisted that some of the maps be reserved from public view throughout the nineteenth century. Meanwhile, during the Anglo-American border disputes of the 1840s, the famous Red-lined Map of 1782 was temporarily transferred to the Foreign Office.

Unlike his grandfather and great-grandfather, George III never visited the

Continent or spent any time in his ancestral lands in Northern Germany. Even in Britain, he did not travel outside the south and west of England. He could not know at first hand, therefore, of the Industrial Revolution which was beginning to transform his kingdom. Industry for him was the prosperous clothing country near Stroud. However, a monarch with such an inquiring mind must have been aware that changes were afoot and noticed many of its artefacts about him. When the first iron bridge in the world was constructed at Coalbrookdale, Shropshire, a model of it was presented to him. Some of the King's travels were associated with his illnesses. When he was unwell in the summer of 1788, before his first attack of madness, he took the waters at Cheltenham. From there he visited Gloucester and Worcester. After his recovery in 1789, his brother the Duke of Gloucester lent him his house overlooking the sea at the Dorset resort of Weymouth so that he could relax and indulge in the new fashion for sea-bathing. In due course George III purchased this house and Weymouth was added to the list of royal residences which most years the Royal Family visited. When, during the Napoleonic Wars, a white horse was cut out of the hillside at Osmington, overlooking Wemouth Bay, the figure of the King was added. Though this was after his last visit to the town, he was popularly said to disapprove, not least because it showed him riding away from Weymouth.

This story is typical of many told about the King and these are testimony to his relationship with his subjects. It was a hierarchical age and George III shared the assumptions that underpinned it. It took all Pitt's perseverance to persuade him to ennoble Robert Smith, the son of a banker, as the first Baron Carrington. Good breeding and landed estates were what counted. Commerce was despised as 'trade'. Nevertheless, some of George's most trusted ministers, such as Addington and Eldon, had certainly risen from the ranks of the middle classes. And, above

all, the King was at ease with his people. Not just at Windsor, the King liked to go about alone, or lightly attended. Usually unrecognized, he spoke to many of those he met and took an interest in their concerns. On one of his journeys west, he overtook a farmer driving sheep, and discussed the value of land and the price of sheep and cattle with him. The man asked him if he had happened to see the King and observed, 'Our neighbours say, he's a good sort of man, but dresses very plain.' To which the King replied, 'Aye, as *plain* as you see me now.' Then there was the old woman he came across working alone in a field, who explained that everyone else had gone off to see the King but that she was too poor to afford the holiday. At which George III, while tipping her, exclaimed that she might tell them that the King had come to see her.

Many of these tales may not have been true but the fact that they were believed demonstrates the widespread affection for the person of the King.

They would not have been
told about George II or
George IV. Unlike them,
George III demonstrated an
affinity with those he ruled.
When at Salisbury Cathedral
he desired to make a
substantial contribution to
the restoration of the spire
and, not being recognized,
was asked what name should
be put in the book, it was said he replied: 'Oh! – a gentleman of Berkshire.' It was
for gestures like these that the King was loved. In 1791 Fanny Burney heard from
a baker woman of Sidmouth of the celebrations in the town on the George III's
recovery from illness two years before. Apart from the feasting laid on for the
poor by the gentry, there had been a portrait of the King 'drest up all in gold &
Lawrels, & they put un in a Coach & Eight Horses, & carried un about: & all the
grand Gentlemen in the Town, & all abouts, come in their own carriages to join.
And they had the finest band of music in all England, singing God Save the
King, & every soul joined in the Chorus, – & all because not so much for a
being he was a King, but because they said as a was such a worthy Gentleman,
& that the like of un was never known in this nation before.'

   Not least of the features that helped to make George III the father
of his people was that he himself was so obviously a family man. Indeed, the
nineteenth-century scribbler Captain Gronow characterized him as 'that obstinate
but domestic monarch'. The birth of his heir, the future George IV, in 1762 was,

of course, a matter of state and the young prince was put on display to the aristocracy for six afternoons as he was rocked by strings of gold lace attached to his cradle. Fourteen more children followed but this was not merely a matter of dynastic or biological necessity. The King loved children, his own or other people's. When his younger offspring had whooping cough in 1785 he fussed over them and, though neither the Queen nor he had had the disease and were therefore at risk of catching it, he could not bear that they be sent away as his elder sons, the Prince of Wales and Duke of York, had been. Dorothy Wordsworth, the sister of the poet, who met the Royal Family on the terrace at Windsor, remarked that 'The King's good temper shews itself in no instance so much as in his affection for children.' He had stopped to play with her young cousins, 'who though not acquainted with the new-fangled doctrines of liberty and equality, thought a king's stick as fair game as any other man's, and that the princesses were not better than mere Cousin Dollys'. Fanny Burney judged him 'one of the most tender fathers in the world'. His consort had a similar reputation. A rhyme of 1779 declared: 'The Queen, they say, / Attends her nursery every day, / And, like a common mother, shares / In all her infants' little cares.' Like all parents of that age, though they were more fortunate in this respect than many, they had to cope as best they could with the death of children. When Prince Octavius died aged four in 1783, his heartbroken father observed, 'There will be no heaven for me if Octavius is not there.' The new east window of St George's Chapel at Windsor portraying the Resurrection contained an image of the young prince. Another favourite was George III's youngest daughter, Princess Amelia. Many thought her fatal illness in 1810 precipitated the King's final mental collapse.

The education of a monarch's children is always fraught with difficulty.

'The King's good temper shews
itself in no instance so much as
in his affection for children.'

George III and Queen Charlotte started out well enough. On the birth of the
Prince of Wales the estimable Lady Charlotte Finch was appointed Governess of
the Royal Nursery and stayed with the Royal Family for thirty years. Though
there were writing masters and any number of tutors it was she who taught at
least some of the children to read. She also introduced newfangled toys, such as
some of the earliest jigsaws ever to be made. Following royal custom, when the
boys reached seven or eight they were taken in pairs and given their own
households. A memorandum of 1776 by the Duke of Montagu, the then
Governor of the royal children, reveals that they breakfasted at nine-thirty a.m.
on milk and toast, dined at three p.m. on plain meat and fish, followed by fruit,
though twice a week they were allowed ices and coffee, and had supper at eight-
thirty. The King felt that as a boy he had been too sheltered from the world.
Consequently, with the exception of the Prince of Wales, when they were old
enough all his other surviving sons were sent away. Frederick, Duke of York,
who was his father's favourite, spent 1781 to 1787 in Germany, mostly in
Hanover. William was destined for the navy, which he joined in 1779. Edward was
in Hanover in 1785–86. Finally, in 1786, Ernest, Augustus and Adolphus were sent
to study at Göttingen. In contrast, however, the King and Queen were possessive
of their daughters, who increasingly began to feel that they were imprisoned in
a nunnery. Only the eldest, Charlotte, who became the wife of Duke Frederick
of Württemberg in 1797, married before their brother became Regent in 1811.

For all the love and care lavished on the Princes, as they grew up they
proved a constant embarrassment to their father. He had urged them to 'become
of credit to their family and of utility to their country'. In later years, the Duke
of Wellington was to remark bluntly that they were millstones round the neck of
the nation. They lacked George III's moral seriousness and sense of duty and all

Alfred. Octav. Sopt. Mary. Adolph. Aug. Eliz. Err

died. Aug 1782.

Amelia
born Aug. 1783.

19. Edw. P.J.Roy. W.Hen. Fred. P.Wales Charl. Geo.III.

1781

were accident prone. Frederick, the 'Grand Old Duke of York' of the nursery
rhyme, was one of the more competent but even he had to resign as
Commander-in-Chief of the Army when his mistress was accused of selling
military commissions. All parents are hostages to fortune where their children are
concerned and in this, as much else, George III was particularly ill-served by fate.
He must have found the private lives of his sons particularly painful.

What made it worse was that the Prince of Wales turned out as he did. The
future George IV possessed no mean intellect and an outstanding appreciation of
the arts. Unfortunately, his selfishness outweighed all his good qualities. His only
real concern was his own gratification. Like all Princes of Wales, and his father
had not been blameless in this respect, he went into opposition to Government.
Some thought that his greatest talent was for spending money. His debts were
soon prodigious. After a succession of mistresses, in 1785 he secretly married
Mrs Fitzherbert. This was not only a breach of the Royal Marriage Act but, since
she was a Roman Catholic, under the law as it stood should have debarred him
from the throne. However, he simply denied that any marriage had taken place.
George III was under no illusions about his heir. He knew by then his son had
sought to have himself made Regent. No less galling, while he himself scrimped
and saved, he had to pay many of the Prince of Wales's bills. Soon, however, other
means had to be found to support the Prince, who by the 1790s, in consequence
of his extravagances, owed well over half a million pounds. The King, who was
eager to safeguard the succession, obviously thought that marriage might help to
steady the young man. At the same time, the increased grant it would bring from
Parliament to support his wife would secure his debts. The Prince was thinking
along similar lines. The bride he selected was his cousin, Princess Caroline of
Brunswick-Wolfenbüttel. The marriage duly took place on 8 April 1795.

This, which should have opened a new era of happiness in the Royal Family, only increased its woes. If the Prince was far from an ideal husband, the Princess was certainly not an ideal wife. Vulgar and headstrong, Caroline was totally lacking in judgement. Husband and wife seem to have taken an instant dislike to one another. Rumour had it that the marriage had lasted only a single night, just long enough for the Princess to conceive. Certainly, after the birth of their daughter, the Princess Charlotte, on 7 January 1796 matters soon reached crisis point. The Prince demanded a separation. The King pointed out what his son so blithely disregarded: 'You seem to look on your disunion with the Princess as merely of a private nature, and totally put out of sight that as heir apparent of the Crown your marriage is a public act.' It was to no avail. A formal separation took place and the Princess left Carlton House and went to live in various mansions in south-east London. There she surrounded herself with children of indeterminate origin, at least one of whom, William Austin, was rumoured to be her illegitimate son. In 1806 George III was forced to commission 'the delicate investigation' into the rumours, which proved groundless though largely her own fault. The King, while aware of his daughter-in-law's failings, always treated her kindly and ensured that she had access to her daughter, in whom he took immense pride. His mental incapacity after 1810 spared him any further involvement in this sorry tale. He may never have known that the young Princess Charlotte died in childbirth in 1817, occasioning an outpouring of national grief only to be surpassed by that on his own death. Astonishingly, at that point, fifty-seven years into George III's reign, she had been his only legitimate grandchild. What he undoubtedly did know, which must have grieved him deeply, was that some of his own popularity arose from the deep unpopularity of his son. He must have feared that the Prince of Wales would undo everything for which he had striven.

6

His derangement ... came out of
the blue. It was preceded by a short
illness, which gave no hint of what
was to follow.

Madness and death
1788–1820

On 25 October 1810 Britain was *en fête* and London was illuminated. The whole country was celebrating the King's Golden Jubilee, the fiftieth anniversary of his accession to the throne. George III was seventy-two. Already he had reigned longer than any British monarch since Edward III. Wherever in the world his subjects were gathered, there were dinners, entertainments and toasts in his honour. *The Times* reported a particularly brilliant show in Lisbon, which the King's troops were guarding against the French at the time, with the ships in the Tagus firing royal salutes, while on land the British merchants gave dinners and at the Opera a gala ended with the display of a beautiful transparency of the King, lit from behind and flanked by troops who presented arms during a rousing performance of the national anthem. 'Every one in the house stood up when it was singing, and the utmost respect and veneration for our revered Monarch was testified.'

George III was now, however, clearly an old man, with many of the ailments of age. In 1804 he developed a cataract in his right eye and in 1805 one began to form in his left. His sight became so poor that he could not even see that the ink on the nib he was writing with had run out. Pitt suggested he co-opt Sir Herbert Taylor, the secretary of his son, the Duke of York, to assist him. It was the first time he had had any secretarial help with his massive workload. In fact, the perception of his decline was such that in many parts of the realm, the anniversary celebrations had been held at the start of his fiftieth regnal year in October 1809 for fear that he might not live another twelve months. Fate was to mock both the King and his subjects in the cruellest possible way. He was to live on for nine years but the very day of the Jubilee was to be effectively the last of his reign. It witnessed the final onset of the terrible illness which had haunted him for the previous twenty years.

Sunday Nov. 9th 10 in ye Morning.

Dr. Warren begs the favor of ye 60
Bp. of Carlisle, to acquaint the Arch
ishop of Canterbury, that an amend
ent came on with respect to His
Majesty's fever, last night; that his
Majesty became quiet & slept three
ours at different times; but Dr.
arren is very sorry to add that, the
pulse was nearly quiet, this Morn.
at 8 o'Clock; the other unfortunate
cumstance remains, as before.

My Dear Lord, His Majesty's pulse is 78
Morning — scarcely any fever — two
in sleep by snatches in the night — but
rambling precisely as before — Queen's

The one thing everyone thinks they know about King George, apart from
his loss of the American colonies, is that he went mad. The malady had first
afflicted him in 1788. Before that, apart from a serious bout of illness in 1765, his
general health had been good. His constitution was robust. He thought nothing
of riding between London and Kew and would regularly spend whole days in the
saddle hunting, which was his favourite diversion. Indeed, such was his stamina
and energy that he often succeeded in exhausting his courtiers and servants. His
derangement, therefore, came out of the blue. It was preceded by a short illness,
which gave no hint of what was to follow.

On 11 June 1788 George III reviewed the Duke of York's regiment on
Wimbledon Common. On his return to Kew he was bilious and seized with such
agonizing stomach cramps that he was forced to go to bed to experience any
relief. He was ill for about a fortnight. Everyone put it down to the hot weather.
Lord Fauconberg, a Lord of the Bedchamber, offered the King the loan of his
house, Bays Hill Lodge, at Cheltenham. Though not as famous or popular as Bath,
Cheltenham had its own spa and the waters were thought to be particularly good
for bilious complaints. The King closed the current session of Parliament on
11 July. It was not to meet again until late November. The following day, at seven
o'clock in the morning, the Royal Family set out from Windsor, breakfasting at
Nuneham Courtenay outside Oxford and reaching their destination in the early
afternoon. George III spent a month at Cheltenham, returning to Windsor on
16 August. It was all a great success. 'Never did schoolboys enjoy their holydays
equal to what we have done our little excursion,' wrote the Queen. The King
was free of ministers and even of a military escort. He and the Queen toured the
locality without any ceremony and the King chatted freely to any of his subjects
he came across, some of whom were quite oblivious of his identity. He thought

the waters had done him much good. Cheltenham's reputation was greatly enhanced, but for the King it was a false dawn.

On the night of 16–17 October, George III was again taken ill. He was bilious, had violent pains in the stomach and cramp in the legs. He was given purges by his doctors and laudanum to dull the pain. This time his illness was ascribed to his not changing his stockings which had got wet. By the 22nd the King was intermittently delirious. However, he made heroic efforts to keep going. On the 24th he insisted on holding his levee at St James's to scotch rumours that he was seriously ill – 'to stop further lies and any fall of the stocks' – but it had the opposite effect and Pitt was seriously alarmed at his condition. The next day the King left Kew for Windsor. There he grew steadily worse. His agitation of spirits increased and he himself remarked that he could not control his ceaseless talking. That he was conscious his illness was overwhelming him made his sufferings far worse. To Lady Effingham he said, 'you see me, all at once, an old man'. More ominously, he observed to the Queen, 'Then you are prepared for [the] worst.' But nothing could have prepared either of them for what was to come.

His situation was rapidly deteriorating. On 3 November he wrote to Pitt to show him that he could still sign warrants though he admitted he was unable to read the despatches. He was not to write again to his Prime Minister for four months. By 5 November George III was deranged. That night the Queen refused to sleep with him. She did not do so again for five months. Meanwhile his delirium increased. On the 9th there were rumours in London that he had died but as one peer wrote from Windsor the King's state 'seems worse than a thousand deaths'. He was likely to live but without his wits. It was becoming urgent that some announcement be made to his subjects and the first public

bulletin was issued on 18 November. What they were not told was that the King
was confined to two rooms and restrained either by being wrapped in sheets or
strapped in a strait-jacket, or waistcoat as it was called in the parlance of the age.
He talked ceaselessly. He believed London had been flooded and wanted to sail
there in his yacht. He also thought that he had seen Hanover through Herschel's
telescope. On the 29th he was removed to Kew where it was hoped he could be
kept out of the public eye, and which was also more convenient for the London
doctors. On 5 December Dr Willis arrived.

Francis Willis and his family cast a heavy shadow over the illnesses of
George III. Willis himself had started as a clergyman and had been Vice-Principal
of Brasenose College, Oxford. In middle life he had studied medicine and
become physician to a hospital in Lincoln. He ran a private madhouse at
Greatford near Stamford – his patients, or rather their families, paid a minimum
of four guineas a week – and had built up a formidable reputation for the
handling of the insane. As were most 'mad doctors' at the time, he was an
exponent of the 'terrific' system, based on terrifying patients into submission
by the use of coercion and restraints. It is clear he was a formidable character.
Even a politician such as Addington, who came to rely on the Willis family,
regarded him as 'rough and violent', and he soon got the better of George III's
senior physicians. These viewed him with disdain, both because of his speciality
and because he was not a member of the Royal College of Physicians. Within
a short time he had effectively excluded them from the sickroom and taken over
complete management of the King. Throughout the day there were three of
Willis's men with him at all times, and two at night. George III had disliked him
from the very beginning. When the Doctor arrived he had told him: 'You have
quitted a profession I have always loved [the Church], & You have Embraced one

I most heartily detest.' Unperturbed, Willis unctuously replied that Jesus Christ went about healing the sick, but the King had his measure. 'Yes, yes, but he had not 700l [pounds] a year for it.'

Though the King was certainly deranged at times, for the next two months Willis, his sons and helpers put the hapless monarch through a regime that would have broken the strongest of men. Blisters were applied to his legs. Emetics to provoke vomiting were secretly administered to him. He was made to sleep in a strait-jacket, with his legs tied to the bedposts. On the 24 January a restraining chair was introduced. The King with grim humour called it his Coronation Chair. In this he would be secured and his mouth gagged. This silenced his enraged protestations as Dr Willis lectured him. It is little wonder that in one of his disturbed periods George III meditated fantastical plans of escape, making extravagant promises of reward to any who would help him. In his more rational moments, he prayed to be restored to his senses or die.

While the King was fighting for his sanity at Kew, the political world likewise was in turmoil. Separate committees of the Lords and Commons had examined the doctors in December. In January they examined them again. They were driven less by concern for the King than political self-interest. If the King did not recover, the Prince of Wales would become Regent. The Prince was in opposition to Government. Even with a restricted Regency, everyone assumed he would turn out the King's ministers and bring in the Whigs. The doctors, therefore, became political pawns. Dr Willis, who claimed confidently that the King would recover, was asserted to be an agent of the ministers. Those doctors who thought the King would not recover were seen as supporters of the opposition. This was unfair to Sir George Baker, the King's senior physician, who was genuinely perplexed by his master's illness. Of Dr Richard Warren, on the

The King remarked simply, 'My Lord,
I have twice read over the evidence of
the physicians on my case, and if I can
stand that, I can stand anything.'

other hand, it was an entirely accurate description. He was actually sending secret bulletins to the Prince of Wales. Meanwhile, legislation was in train to establish a Regency.

It was not to be needed. Throughout February 1789 George III's health steadily improved. On the 3rd he was allowed to shave himself for the first time in three months. On the 17th he was able to see the Lord Chancellor, Thurlow. The third and final reading of the Regency Bill was scheduled for the 19th. On that day the Chancellor rose from the Woolsack and announced to the Lords that it would be inappropriate to proceed with it. On the 23rd the King saw the Prince of Wales and the Duke of York and, on the following day, his Prime Minister, Pitt. On the 26th George III himself ordered that the public bulletins on his health should be discontinued. His domestic arrangements began to return to some semblance of normality. On 3 March he and the Queen took up life together again and on the 14th returned to Windsor. The Willises insisted on keeping the King under some sort of observation for a month. They finally left Windsor at the end of March. Parliament voted Dr Francis Willis a pension of £1,000 for twenty-one years and the King presented him with a gold watch. The country for its part rejoiced. The windows in all the major London thoroughfares were illuminated on 9 March and the Queen arranged a private illumination of Kew Palace, displaying images of the King, Providence, Health and Britannia. On St George's Day, 23 April, the King attended a Service of Thanksgiving for his recovery at St Paul's Cathedral. The Archbishop of Canterbury had tried to dissuade him, fearing the strain would be too much. The King remarked simply, 'My Lord, I have twice read over the evidence of the physicians on my case, and if I can stand that, I can stand anything.'

The King's illness had come out of nowhere and for the next eleven years

The Grand Procession to St Paul's on
St George's Day 1789, to celebrate the
King's recovery.
Guildhall Library, Corporation of London

George III was free of it. In February 1801 it returned. By the 21st the King was
himself so aware of his state that he prayed he might die rather than lose his
sanity. The next day the Royal Family summoned Dr Willis's son, Dr John Willis,
and the King was confined. The Willises sent to a Hoxton madhouse keeper for
four men to attend the King. Pitt, who was leaving office, again contemplated a
Regency. By the end of the month the King was in a coma and it looked as if he
would die. Instead, he rallied and on 14 March he was well enough to receive the

Iolland's Caricature Exhibition Rooms may be seen the Largest Collection of Political and other humorous Prints admittance 1 Shil

seals of office from Pitt on his resignation. By the end of the month George was demanding that the Willises go. On 17 April they left. They had, however, come to regard the King as almost their private possession, a living testament to their medical skills. Their care of him brought them prominence, prosperity and power, the latter not least because they controlled access to him. At this point the Queen and the Royal Family played into their hands. Faced again with coping with the King and uncertain about his mental condition, they panicked and recalled the mad doctors. The Willises planned to detain the King at Buckingham House on the 18th but he left for Kew before they could strike. They rode off in pursuit. Next day they apprehended him at the Prince of Wales's House at Kew and kept him in close confinement at Kew Palace for a month. This extraordinary episode shows the hold they had obtained over the political establishment. Scarcely surprisingly, George III was outraged. He told the Reverend Thomas Willis, another of Dr Willis's sons, whom until now he had quite liked, 'Sir, I will never forgive you whilst I live.' Finally, on 19 May he simply refused to sign any more documents unless he were released and so secured his freedom.

In 1804 he suffered a third visitation of the sickness. In the middle of January he contracted what seemed a cold, again attributed to wet clothes. By the second week of February, his 'fever' and its symptoms had reached crisis point. With grim inevitability Addington, the Prime Minister, called in the Willises. They had received a further £10,000 for their services in 1801 and must have thought themselves indispensable. On 13 February they arrived at Buckingham House to take charge of the King but, this time, they were to be rebuffed. So great was the King's loathing of them that he had exacted a promise from his sons that he would never again be committed to their care. Accordingly, the Dukes of Kent and Cumberland physically barred their way to the King. It did him little good. Instead Addington turned to Dr Samuel Simmons, physician to St Luke's Hospital for Lunaticks. In fact, George III began slowly to recover, but this did not prevent Simmons from applying the strait-jacket. Astonishingly, in the midst of all this the King was well enough to change his Prime Ministers. On 10 May Pitt kissed hands. The Prince of Wales, who thought he should be Regent, was not the only person to comment on 'so extraordinary a circumstance as a King of England whilst exercising his Regal powers being kept under any personal restraint'. On 20 July George moved from Kew to Windsor and freedom, though Simmons did not depart until 20 August. The King was still agitated and irritable. The saddest consequence of this illness was a rift between the King and his wife. Queen Charlotte decided she could take no more. After 1804 she and George III led separate lives.

The nature of the King's illness perplexed his subjects at the time and has been a matter of debate ever since. As Boswell remarked of Samuel Johnson's fears on the subject, in the Age of Reason, madness was 'the evil most to be dreaded'. Madness and depression were often confounded and Dr George Cheyne wrote a popular treatise on melancholy as *The English Malady*, to be explained by the weather. George III was not, however, melancholic but periodically deranged. Nor was he the only European monarch in this period to suffer mental incapacity. His first cousin and brother-in-law, Christian VII of Denmark, was an imbecile, while Maria I of Portugal suffered the dubious honour of becoming another patient of Dr Francis Willis. The King's illnesses were variously explained by his supposed vices, obstinacy and pride, or his virtues. Dr Willis instanced 'Twenty-seven years ... [of] weighty Business, severe Exercise, and too great Abstemiousness, and little Rest'. Minor physical causes were attributed to the onset of the attacks, while many attributed the severity of these to stress.

Anyone who has had the final responsibility for even a small enterprise can imagine something of the strains imposed by kingship. George III certainly felt these and described them graphically. In 1782, at the end of the American War of Independence, he expressed the consciousness of 'a mind truly tore to pieces'. In 1783, when faced with the reality of the Fox–North Coalition, he observed: 'my sorrow may prove fatal to my health if I remain long in this thraldom'. As his age increased and with it his apparent predisposition to bouts of insanity,

A bulletin, dated 19 October 1811,
in the one of the journals kept by
Dr Robert Willis during the early part
of the King's third illness from 1810
to 1812.
*The British Library, Add. MS 41733 H,
ff.18v–19*

his ministers grew more and more anxious lest the cares of office precipitate an attack. In 1804 when he was going out of office Addington remarked, at a time when the King was indeed unwell, 'to keep his [the King's] health safe is the cause of the country'. The following year when Britain's allies Prussia and Russia were discovered to have included a secret clause in a treaty for the annexation of Hanover by the former, Pitt dared not tell the King for fear it would kill him or drive him mad. However, George III does not seem to have had what would

today be called 'a nervous disposition'. Fanny Burney, discovering that he was a
keen reader of the newspapers with all their disobliging comments, remarked that
he 'must then have the most unvexing temper in the world not to run wild'.
There is also the evidence of George's calmness after attempts on his life. In 1786
Margaret Nicholson tried to stab the King with a dessert knife. In 1800 James
Hadfield fired at him in Drury Lane Theatre. On both occasions the King's
composure and self-control were remarkable and much remarked. And if the
burdens of his high state had been responsible for George III's madness, it would
be difficult to explain the illness of 1788 which struck at a time of comparative
political tranquillity.

So if it was not stress which caused the madness of King George, what was
it? Contemporaries simply did not know. It was this which so agitated his family,
his doctors and his ministers. Since he seemed to be the victim of a malady that
was beyond their comprehension, they had no real idea of how it should be

treated, nor any reliable way of predicting if and when it might strike again. No wonder their panic was almost palpable. It was to be almost one hundred and fifty years after the King's death before anyone was to advance a reasonably convincing diagnosis. In the 1960s Ida Macalpine and Richard Hunter, reading through the medical notes which survived on the King's illness, observed that these mentioned in passing that his urine was often dark or bloody, and left a blue stain on the vessel when it was poured away. They therefore postulated that George III suffered from porphyria, a rare condition only recognized in the 1930s. This is an excess in the body of the substance which colours red blood cells. The resulting chemical imbalance poisons the nervous system and leads to violent pain, physical weakness and mental derangement. The hypothesis of Macalpine and Hunter accords with all the known facts of the case and has been widely accepted since. None of this, of course, could have been guessed in the King's lifetime. For contemporaries and succeeding generations George III was quite simply 'mad', with all that implied, and this necessarily coloured their judgements. For example, Baron Stockmar witnessing Queen Victoria's violent temper thought that she had inherited her grandfather's insanity and he even discerned it in the future Edward VII as well.

In 1810, the onset of the King's final period of madness was thought to have been caused by his intense distress at the plight of his youngest daughter, Princess Amelia, who was dying of tuberculosis. Symptoms of agitation had appeared on 22 October and by the time of his Golden Jubilee on the 25th it was very evident that all was not well. This time his doctors were determined to avoid restraint if they could and Dr Simmons, who presented himself at Windsor with his assistants, went away in dudgeon when he was refused sole management of the King. Unfortunately, early in November George III's condition worsened and he was strapped in a strait-jacket for over a week. The Privy Council, Lords and Commons took evidence from the physicians and on 19 December Spencer Perceval, the Prime Minister, told the Prince of Wales that he intended to introduce legislation establishing a regency. However, it looked for a time as if this might not be necessary. Over Christmas the King was so ill it was thought he would die. It would have been happier for him if he had, but his iron constitution carried him through. In January the Regency Bill was introduced. It had its third reading on 31 January 1811 and on 5 February the Lord Chancellor sealed the commission giving it the Royal Assent. The next day the Prince of Wales took the oath of office. The Regency had begun.

Ironically, by this time George III's health, which always had the power to disconcert, appeared much improved. The Prince Regent himself fell dangerously ill and some wag suggested that the King be made regent for the Regent. Tragically, George III himself expected to resume the reins of power. However, now that the momentous step, first discussed over twenty years before, of installing a regent had at last been taken, no one was willing to put their trust in the vagaries of the King's condition. Whether it was chagrin at this rebuff or the natural course of his disease, he relapsed, indulging in fantastical plans for rebuilding his palaces and instituting a female order of chivalry – this latter considered an obvious sign of insanity! All the old symptoms reasserted themselves – a fast pulse, sweating, sleeplessness, weakness of the limbs, colic, constipation. A year later, six weeks after the beginning of the Parliamentary session in January 1812, the Prince Regent assumed full royal powers, as allowed for in the Regency Act of 1811, parliament judging that there was no longer any hope of the King's recovery.

The remainder of George III's life was passed in a few rooms at Windsor

Castle. On his better days he might be taken for a walk on the castle terrace. The care of the King's person had been vested, by the Act of Regency, in Queen Charlotte and a council including the Archbishop of Canterbury. After her death on 17 November 1818, it passed to Frederick, Duke of York. Dr Robert Darling Willis had been early involved in the care of the King – old Dr Willis had died in 1807 – and in November 1811, his brother, Dr John Willis was reintroduced much to the King's fury. By 1812 the Willises had again all but excluded the other physicians. The nation, meanwhile, lived in expectation of the monarch's death. A careful Scottish lady Mrs Grant of Rothiemurchus, fearing that mourning would rocket in price, bought up a large quantity of black bombazine fabric at a sale. She had to find other uses for it. Though dead to the world, the King lived on.

The passing years saw momentous events. In 1812, the Prime Minister, Spencer Perceval was shot dead by a madman. In 1814 the abdication of Napoleon was followed by the visit to London of the allied sovereigns. The same year the capital celebrated the centenary of the House of Hanover. In 1815 Wellington defeated Napoleon at Waterloo. In 1817 to the grief of the whole nation George III's granddaughter, and after her father, his heiress, Princess Charlotte of Wales, died in childbirth. Did the King know any of this? What senses he still had were fading. Almost blind, in 1817 his hearing also failed. The last picture of George III shows a King-Lear-like figure, with staring eyes and long white flowing hair. By the end of 1819 his iron constitution began to falter. Finally, at just after half past eight on the evening of 29 January 1820, without apparent suffering, he died. As it was expressed in the sonorous words proclaiming his son and successor King, 'it hath pleased Almighty God to call to his mercy our late Sovereign Lord King George the Third, of blessed memory'.

Though George III had in reality already been no more than a memory for
a decade, it was one his subjects held dear. The details of his passing excited not
only profound regret but also enormous interest. On 1 February the Lord
Chamberlain took charge of the King's body, which was bound in linen prepared
with wax. On the 3rd his coffins arrived at Windsor from France and Banting's in
St James Street and he was placed in them. The inmost one was mahogany, lined
with the richest white satin. This was sealed in a lead coffin and the whole
enclosed in another mahogany coffin. The King's body lay in state in the Audience
Chamber at Windsor on the 15th and 16th, raised on a temporary dais under a

Cruikshanks del

FUNERAL PROCE

N OF GEORGE III.

rich black canopy, and surmounted by the Imperial Crown and the Crown of
Hanover. So many people descended on Windsor to pay their respects that it was
impossible for all of them to secure bed or board for themselves, or stabling for
their horses. Many were of the humblest class. None was refused admittance.

The funeral itself took place on the evening of 16 February 1820. It was
Ash Wednesday, the first day of Lent, always an occasion of solemn fasting. In
London and elsewhere, all shops were shut and the churches were full. Even
nonconformist chapels and synagogues held services. Throughout the day at
Windsor signal guns were fired at five-minute intervals and mourning bells tolled.
At six o'clock in the evening all who had procured tickets were admitted to the
precincts of the castle and the courtyard was packed with spectators. Although extra
seating had been erected in St George's Chapel, the number of places available for
the general public was so small that sums of fifty guineas were being offered
unsuccessfully for tickets. At seven o'clock guests were admitted to the chapel, but
it was another two hours before the funeral procession bearing the King's coffin
set out from the state apartments. While it was borne towards the chapel, the bands
played over and over again the Dead March from Handel's *Saul* and, as it slowly
proceeded on its way, the flaring torches distributed among the troops lit up both
the faces of the crowd and the towers and battlements of Windsor Castle. The
Chief Mourner was the Duke of York. The coffin was preceded by the Crown of
Hanover and the Imperial Crown. The Duke of Wellington and five other dukes
were pallbearers and the canopy was carried by ten marquesses. In the chapel,
a sumptuous canopy had been erected over the royal vault. The service was
conducted by the Dean of Windsor, assisted by the Archibishop of Canterbury.
At its end, the choir sung the anthem composed by Handel for the funeral of the
King's grandmother, Queen Caroline. After the committal prayer was read the

> 'Thus ended the most awful and
> magnificent ceremony which any
> British subject now living ever
> witnessed in this country; a
> ceremony ... rendered sublime
> by the voluntary and heartfelt
> homage of countless thousands
> of affectionate subjects ...'

coffin sank slowly out of sight into the vault and Sir Isaac Heard, Garter King of Arms, who in 1760 had been one of the heralds who had proclaimed George III King, read out his titles for the last time. Thousands of the public were then admitted so that they could look down and see the coffin.

The Times ventured to capture the mood of the hour: 'Thus ended the most awful and magnificent ceremony which any British subject now living ever witnessed in this country; a ceremony ... rendered sublime by the voluntary and heartfelt homage of countless thousands of affectionate subjects, who had thronged to the last obsequies of their King, not from the idle curiosity of seeing a grand exhibition, but to shed a last tear over the grave of a father and a friend.' None of these had known George III personally but all felt as if they had for, by the end of his life, the King who had gloried in the name of Britain had come to represent for the majority of his subjects the unpretentious virtues and simple pieties that were the lifeblood of the nation. For the few who *had* known him, relief was mingled with the sadness. The last words should be left to the novelist Fanny Burney, who, as a member of Queen Charlotte's household, had come to know George III well. She had hated court life but had deeply admired the King: 'No one ... can live – and breathe – and think; and dare lament that the so good, so pious, so amiable & so exemplary *George the Third* should be gone to his great reward -- should be relieved from those trammels of Earthly machinery that were no longer informed by the faculties that for so many years guided him to all that was Right – should have his soul liberated from the malady of his Brain & freed to enjoy the salubrity of those Regions for which it was fitted, -- nevertheless, no one could have known him as I have known him, in all the private excellencies of his domestic benevolences, – & have shared as well as witnessed them – without feelings of depression & sadness that such a Man is now no more.'

Chronology

1714	Death of Queen Anne. Succession of George I and the House of Hanover
1727	Death of George I and accession of George II
1736	Marriage of Frederick, Prince of Wales, to Augusta of Saxe-Gotha
1738	24 May (old style dating system), 4 June (new style): birth of George III
1745	Second Jacobite Rebellion
1749	22 June: George III created Knight of the Garter
1751	20 March: death of Frederick, Prince of Wales
	20 April: George III created Prince of Wales
1760	25 October: death of George II and accession of George III
1761	8 September: marries Charlotte of Mecklenburg-Strelitz
	22 September: crowned in Westminster Abbey
1762	26 May: Lord Bute appointed Prime Minister
	12 August: birth of George, Prince of Wales (George IV)
	Purchase of Buckingham House
1763	10 February: Peace of Paris ends Seven Years War
	16 April: Grenville succeeds Bute as Prime Minister
1765	March: Grenville's Stamp Act (repealed 1766)
	21 August: birth of William Henry, Duke of Clarence (William IV)
1767	Townshend's Import Duties in America
1770	28 January: Lord North appointed Prime Minister
1772	8 February: death of George III's mother, Augusta, Princess of Wales
1773	16 December: the Boston Tea Party
1775	19 April: the first skirmishes of the American War of Independence at Lexington and Concord
	23 August: George III proclaims the American Colonies to be in a state of rebellion
1776	4 July: American Declaration of Independence
1777	16 October: Burgoyne surrenders at Saratoga
1781	19 October: Cornwallis surrenders at Yorktown
1782	27 March: Rockingham succeeds North as Prime Minister
1783	7 August: birth of Princess Amelia, George III's youngest child
	3 September: Peace of Versailles recognizes American independence
	19 December: Pitt the Younger appointed Prime Minister

1788	July–August: George III visits Cheltenham
	October: onset of the King's first attack of 'madness'
1789	23 April: George III celebrates his recovery at St Paul's Cathedral
	14 July: Storming of the Bastille in Paris
1793	21 January: execution of Louis XVI
	1 February: France declares war on Britain
1795	8 April: Prince of Wales marries Caroline of Brunswick-Wolfenbüttel
1796	7 January: birth of Princess Charlotte of Wales
1798	Rebellion and French invasion in Ireland
1801	1 January: union of Great Britain and Ireland as the United Kingdom
	February–April: George III's second attack of 'madness'
	17 March: Pitt succeeded as Prime Minister by Henry Addington
1802	27 March: Peace of Amiens with France
1803	18 May: renewal of hostilities between Britain and France
1804	February–July: George III's third attack of 'madness'
	10 May: Pitt returns as Prime Minister
1805	13 June: Sir Herbert Taylor appointed Private Secretary
	21 October: Battle of Trafalgar
1806	23 January: death of Pitt
	13 September: death of Charles James Fox
1810	25 October: the King's Golden Jubilee. His illness returns
1811	5 February: Prince of Wales becomes Regent
1815	18 June: Battle of Waterloo ends the French Wars
1817	6 November: death of Princess Charlotte of Wales
1818	17 November: death of Queen Charlotte
1819	24 May: birth of Princess Victoria of Kent (Queen Victoria)
1820	29 January: death of George III at Windsor
	16 February: funeral and interment at St George's Chapel, Windsor
1823	George IV presents George III's Library to the nation
1831	George III's statue, the Copper Horseman, erected at Windsor
1997	George III's Library moved to the new British Library building

Further reading

There are many books and articles which explore the history of George III and his times. The following are a selection.

John Brooke, *King George III* (Constable, London, 1972), remains the best introduction to the King's life and reign, though it concentrates on the period before 1789. Other general studies of the King and his consort are: Stanley Ayling, *George the Third* (Collins, London, 1972); Christopher Hibbert, *George III, A Personal History* (Viking, London, 1998); and Olwen Hedley, *Queen Charlotte* (John Murray, London, 1975).

The King's correspondence is edited by Sir John Fortescue, *The Correspondence of King George III*, 6 vols. (Frank Cass & Co, London, 1967). A more approachable selection of his letters appears in Bonamy Dobrée (ed.), *The Letters of King George III* (Cassell, London, 1935).

The King's illness is discussed at length in Ida Macalpine and Richard Hunter, *George III and the Mad-Business* (Allen Lane, London, 1969).

The context of the King's reign is provided by Roy Porter, *English Society in the Eighteenth Century* (Penguin, Harmondsworth, 1990); J. C. D. Clark, *English Society 1688-1832* (Cambridge, 1985); and Linda Colley, *Britons: forging the nation 1707-1837* (Pimlico, London, 1994).

The Oxford Dictionary of National Biography (2004) contains the latest research on the lives of the King's most distinguished subjects. More detailed information on leading politicians can be found in the relevant volumes of *The History of Parliament*: Sir Lewis Namier and John Brooke (eds.), *The House of Commons 1754-1790* (London, 1964) and R. G. Thorne (ed.), *The House of Commons 1790-1820* (Secker & Warburg, London, 1986).

An excellent history of the royal buildings in this period is provided by J. Mordaunt Crook and M. H. Port in *The History of the King's Works, Vol. VI 1782-1851* (H.M.S.O., London, 1973).

A much fuller list of books and articles will be found in two volumes of the *Bibliography of British History*: S. Pargellis and D. J. Medley (eds.), *The Eighteenth Century 1714-1789* (Harvester Press, Hassocks, 1977) and Lucy M. Brown and Ian R. Christie (eds.) *1789-1851* (Clarendon Press, Oxford, 1977).

Index